Aeschylus

Prometheus Bound

Aeschylus

Prometheus Bound

Translated,
with Introduction and Notes, by

Deborah H. Roberts

Hackett Publishing Company, Inc.
Indianapolis/Cambridge

15 14 13 12   1 2 3 4 5 6 7

For further information, please address
   Hackett Publishing Company, Inc.
   P.O. Box 44937
   Indianapolis, Indiana 46244-0937

   www.hackettpublishing.com

Cover design by Brian Rak
Interior design and composition by Elizabeth L. Wilson
Printed at Sheridan Books, Inc.

Library of Congress Cataloging-in-Publication Data
Aeschylus.
   [Prometheus bound. English]
   Prometheus bound / Aeschylus ; translated, with introduction and notes,
by Deborah Roberts.
      p. cm.
   Includes bibliographical references.
   ISBN 978-1-60384-190-0 (pbk.) — ISBN 978-1-60384-191-7 (cloth)
   1. Prometheus (Greek deity)—Drama. 2. Aeschylus. Prometheus bound.
I. Roberts, Deborah H. II. Title.
   PA3825.P8 2012
   882'.01—dc23   2011044754

The paper used in this publication meets the minimum requirements of
American National Standard for Information Sciences—Permanence of
Paper for Printed Library Materials, ANSI Z39.48–1984.

Contents

Introduction

Prometheus is best known to modern readers as the Greek god who stole fire from the other gods, gave it to human beings, and was cruelly punished for that theft, tortured daily by an eagle that ate his ever-regenerating liver. This story has made him doubly an emblem of resistance to power, since he embodies both wily subversion and stubborn endurance. It also associates him closely with human beings; the gift of fire, which in many accounts gives rise to and stands for technological achievement and creativity, makes him our benefactor, while his punishment makes him our fellow sufferer, subject as mortals are to the will of the ruling gods. *Prometheus Bound* dramatizes a part of the myth of Prometheus that falls between the theft and the well-known punishment and looks backward and forward to other events. Immobilized by his chains, the god can see beyond them, and takes his hearers traveling through distant regions and into past and future as he tells his own story and the stories of others.

The Play and the Myth

Prometheus Bound takes place far earlier in the chronology of Greek myth than any other surviving Greek tragedy. The war between the Olympian gods and the Titans, children of Uranus (Sky) and Gaia (Earth), has just ended. Zeus, king of the Olympians, has defeated his father, the Titan Cronus, who had previously overthrown his own father, and is newly established on the throne. Whereas in other plays the rule of the Olympian gods is a given (if sometimes hard to understand or to accept), here it is only a very recent fact, and could still, perhaps, be reversed. The play's central character, the Titan Prometheus, is

Zeus' former ally, the subverter of his authority, and the prophet of his potential downfall.

Prometheus' theft of fire precedes the action of *Prometheus Bound*; the coming of the eagle that will devour his liver, announced in the concluding scene, follows the play's action by a long expanse of years. In this play, Prometheus is initially punished not by the torment of the eagle but by the agony and the isolation of his binding, and it is his response to the experience of this imprisonment that will bring on him the further punishment we expect.

It is more than likely that the play's fifth-century BCE audience would also have expected this further punishment by the eagle, since it is one of the oldest elements of the myth, part of the story as told by the archaic Greek poet Hesiod, our earliest source.[1] In his *Theogony*, Hesiod tells the story of the origins and genealogy of the gods. He also recounts Cronus' violent overthrow of his father, Uranus, the victory of Zeus and the younger gods over the Titans, and the failure of other threats to Zeus' rule. Hesiod's Prometheus, here the son of the Titans Iapetus and Clymene, is a divine trickster who allies himself with mortals (minor players in this story) in opposition to Zeus; he can never finally succeed, and the help he gives mortals brings on them further suffering. To emphasize the power of Zeus, Hesiod begins his account with the binding and torment of Prometheus, and then describes the events that precede. Prometheus first attempts to deceive Zeus into taking the bones of a sacrificial ox and leaving the meat for mortals. In his anger, Zeus withholds fire from human beings. When Prometheus then steals fire on their behalf, Zeus punishes mortals by sending them (through Prometheus' thoughtless brother Epimetheus) the "beautiful evil" Pandora, and punishes Prometheus by imprisoning him and sending the eagle to torture him. We also learn that Heracles eventually kills the eagle and releases Prometheus, and that this is done with the permission of Zeus.

---

1. Hesiod (who probably lived sometime around 700 BCE) is our earliest Greek source for the story of Prometheus, but there are parallels (or possibly antecedents) in several Near Eastern narratives of creation, divine conflict, and the near-destruction and survival of human beings. See S. West 1994.

Hesiod gives another (somewhat different) account of Prometheus and Pandora in his *Works and Days*, but between Hesiod's poems and *Prometheus Bound* we have no surviving narratives, although there are scattered literary references and a number of visual depictions.[2] It is possible that an element of the story that survives only in later versions, Prometheus' creation of human beings, was already a part of the myth. If so, it would help account for his otherwise unexplained affinity for mortals— an affinity also reflected in the tradition that he is the father of Deucalion, one of two survivors of the great flood that kills all other human beings. The play's Athenian audience would have known the god as the object of local cult worship; he shared with Hephaestus an altar in the outskirts of the city, and an annual torch race was held in his honor.

Almost all Greek tragedies take their plots from a body of continuous myth that is consistent in its broad outlines but varied in detail. It follows that audiences typically had some knowledge of both plot and background, but the playwright might draw on less familiar versions, invent new details, and exclude or downplay elements of the story. In *Prometheus Bound*, Prometheus is the son not of the Titan Clymene but of Earth herself, here identified with the goddess Themis, a personification of divine law who appears in Hesiod's genealogy as Earth's daughter. And Earth's role in the play's background story, though it recalls aspects of her role in Hesiod, is mediated by the son to whom she conveys prophetic knowledge. In the *Theogony*, Earth herself tricks the Titan Cronus on behalf of his children; in *Prometheus Bound*, Earth is said to have told Prometheus that the victory would go to those "superior in trickery," and to have joined him in an alliance with Zeus and the other gods against the Titans.

Prometheus' most important piece of prophetic knowledge represents a variation on another story told by Hesiod. In the *Theogony*, Earth and Sky warn Zeus that his marriage to the goddess Metis (personification of crafty thought) will eventually result in a son who becomes king of gods and men; to avoid this fate he swallows the pregnant Metis, and himself gives birth

---

2. On representations of Prometheus in ancient art, see Podlecki 2005, 37–41.

to Athena from his head. In *Prometheus Bound*, Prometheus knows that if Zeus makes a particular marriage it will result in his overthrow; though this prediction recalls the Metis story, it seems to refer instead to a similar story told by the fifth-century poet Pindar (*Isthmian Odes* 8), in which Themis warns Zeus and Poseidon not to pursue their courtship of the sea-goddess Thetis (later the mother of Achilles), since she is fated to bear a child stronger than his father.

In another departure from Hesiod, Aeschylus has Prometheus give human beings much more than fire or crafts derived specifically from fire; he is the source of all the arts of civilized existence. And this play makes no mention of the deceptive sacrifice or of Pandora, major elements in Hesiod's story that directly lead up to and follow the theft of fire. It's possible that if *Prometheus Bound* was the second play in a trilogy (see below), the Pandora story played some part in the preceding drama, but this seems unlikely, since in Aeschylus' version mortals seem generally to benefit rather than to suffer from Prometheus' intervention in their lives. More surprising than the absence of Pandora is the introduction (as one of Prometheus' visitors) of a different young woman: Io, loved by Zeus, transformed into a cow, and harassed by Zeus' jealous wife Hera. There is no trace in the prior tradition of any encounter between Prometheus and Io, but Aeschylus links their stories.

The Plot

Aeschylus' play, set in the isolated northern region of Scythia, begins with the binding of Prometheus by a reluctant Hephaestus, smith of the gods, under the supervision of Zeus' agents Power and Force. Immobilized and in pain, Prometheus is reduced (if we can call it that) to his powers of speech, sight, and hearing, and to the foreknowledge for which he is said to be named: Prometheus means something like "the one who thinks ahead," "the fore-knower."[3] As the drama proceeds, he speaks

---

3. This was the accepted etymology in antiquity, and is probably correct. Some scholars have argued for other derivations, citing as evidence possibly cognate Sanskrit roots for *fire* or *theft*.

with a series of visitors: the daughters of Ocean, the chorus of this play, who listen sympathetically; Ocean himself, who somewhat pompously offers his condolences and proposes to intervene with Zeus; and Io, wandering the world as a result of Zeus' desire and Hera's hatred.

In the course of these conversations, Prometheus tells his listeners and the audience about events both past and future. He tells how he and his mother came to side with Zeus and the other gods against the Titans; he explains how he subsequently rescued mortals from destruction at Zeus' hands, gave them fire, and transformed their condition, and how this led to his punishment. He describes what other Titans are suffering, and after Io herself has told how her troubles began, he gives a detailed account of the extent of her wanderings, both past and still to come. His narratives are punctuated by expressions of anguish and criticisms of Zeus and the other gods, and his listeners' questions at times force him to comment on or defend his own actions. He also offers an increasingly explicit and gradually shifting prediction of how his own suffering will come to an end, and reveals his knowledge of the marriage that will lead to Zeus' downfall. In response to his assertions about this marriage, he receives one last visitor, Hermes, messenger of the gods. Hermes threatens Prometheus with added punishment—years underground followed by a return to the upper world to be tortured by the eagle—if he will not reveal what he knows. Prometheus refuses to tell, the chorus refuse to abandon him, and as the play ends, the storm that heralds the beginning of his further suffering begins.

Setting: Human and Divine

Prometheus Bound differs from other tragedies not only in being set in the far distant past but also in featuring a protagonist who is a god in a world of gods; the only character in the play identified as mortal is Io, and she is the daughter of a river-divinity. In many Greek tragedies, the gods have an important effect on human action and interaction without actually appearing in the drama; in Sophocles' *Oedipus Tyrannus*, for example, Apollo's oracle and the characters' response to it are central to the unfolding of the plot, but Apollo himself never appears onstage or speaks except through human intermediaries. Where gods do appear, it is usually at the beginning or ending of a play, to explain the background of the story, to anticipate its unfolding, to control its conclusion, or to predict what comes next. There are notable exceptions, among them Aeschylus' *Eumenides* and Euripides' *Bacchae*, where divinities play central roles in the action. But *Prometheus Bound* is unique in another respect. In all other surviving plays the gods are chiefly concerned with human behavior, either toward other humans or toward the gods; in this play, the gods are chiefly concerned with the behavior of the gods, either toward each other or toward human beings.

We might suppose that this difference of setting and character would significantly alter the dynamics of tragedy and the audience's response. But this is only partly true. The fact that the Greek gods are in so many ways like humans means that *Prometheus Bound* shares many issues and themes with tragedies set in the world of humans. Although Prometheus describes the Olympian gods as "the happy," with a distinctive adjective often applied to the divine, immortals are here as capable of pain and suffering as humans; words for grief, misery, and misfortune express Prometheus' own condition, the fate of his fellow Titans, and the prospect of Zeus' fall. Nor is this suffering purely mental or emotional: the text dwells on Prometheus' tortured body and his physical pain.

Among gods as among humans suffering often turns out to follow from acts of injustice and the disruption of familial or social bonds. In this play, two parties, once allies and connected as well by the "terrible strength" of kinship, accuse each other of treachery, wrongdoing, and injustice. For Zeus and the other gods, Prometheus has erred in giving humans a prerogative, fire, "to which they have no right." For Prometheus, who both acknowledges his act as error and claims it as deliberate choice ("I meant to go wrong. I meant to"), Zeus and the other gods have unjustly returned evil for good, mistreating him although he helped them gain power. These claims of wrongdoing occur (as in many human tragedies) in a context of political change and crisis. The characters in this play are ever-conscious of political power ("freedom belongs to nobody but Zeus") and its evolution ("He is harsh, as all those new to power are harsh"), whether they resist or submit to Zeus' authority.

If the world of the gods itself seems not unlike the world of humans in its display of tragic choice and tragic suffering, the play also gives us glimpses of mortal experience and of the treatment of humans at the hands of gods—rather as Aeschylus' *Persians*, a tragedy set at the Persian court during the Persian king's invasion of Greece, is punctuated by glimpses of the Greeks. Prometheus is from the outset of the play strongly associated with humans, and they are a recurring presence in the conversations and narratives that dominate the play. To prevent their destruction, he lost the friendship of Zeus, and he is reminded at several points of their helplessness—a helplessness he could only partially remedy and in some sense now shares. And although he is himself imprisoned in a "wilderness where no mortals live," we learn from the chorus that human beings all over the world mourn for him and for his fellow Titans. Prometheus himself gives a vivid description of human suffering in the state of nature, now mitigated by his gift of various arts and technologies, and his account of Io's past and future wandering provides a kind of virtual tour of various peoples.

In all these examples, we might see human beings simply as a kind of adjunct to the story of Prometheus: victims of his enemy, exemplars of his achievement, mourners for his suffering, markers of his knowledge of space as well as time. But in bringing Io into the story and onstage, Aeschylus provides direct knowledge of a mortal victim of Zeus. Other versions of Io's story make Hera Io's chief tormenter, but though Io several times mentions Hera's role, it is clear that she and Prometheus and the chorus all see Zeus' unwelcome desire and his insistence on her exile from her home as the central causes of her suffering. The arrival of Io offers a kind of mirror of Prometheus' mistreatment in the mistreatment of a helpless human being, her long wandering both a contrast with and an analogue to his long imprisonment in one place.

If, however, the encounter between Prometheus and Io assimilates the experiences of god and human, it also emphasizes the distinction between them. Where Io is mortal, Prometheus will live forever. And where Io must ask what the future will bring, Prometheus knows. Their encounter thus points up two of the basic differences between mortal and human, and two aspects of humanness—mortality and limited knowledge—frequently implicated in the problematic choices and the unforeseen and irretrievable outcomes central to tragedy. How is it possible, we might think, for a central character who is immortal and knows everything—even if he is caught up in the same dilemmas and the same suffering as human beings—to share the irremediable loss and the anguish of belated understanding common to the experience of mortals in Greek tragedy?

Prometheus' immortality explicitly sets him apart from Io, but it is not clear that this is an advantage. The fact that he cannot die may sometimes spur him to resistance ("What should I fear? It's not my fate to die") but it also adds to his agony ("You would find my trials difficult to take / since death's no part of what's in store for me"). His foreknowledge is similarly complex in the role it plays and in how it is valued.

The play makes clear that having knowledge of the future is a mixed gift. Prometheus assists human beings both by giving them the relatively mundane capacity to predict the seasons by reading the stars and by teaching them the "unmapped art" of divination. But the first gift he mentions, even before fire—and the one the chorus call "a great service"—is a kind of cancellation of foreknowledge: he has prevented mortals from foreseeing their deaths. And although he gives in to Io's insistence on learning what further suffering awaits her, when she first asks to know the end of her wanderings he tells her that "not to learn this is better than to learn it." When she asks why he hesitates, he replies, "From no ill will: I'm afraid I'll break your heart."

Prometheus' own knowledge of the future appears at the outset curiously intermittent. Like Io, he asks (in his opening words) where his suffering will end, only to stop himself and assert that since he knows the future "in all its particulars, no pain can surprise me." Even so, however, he expresses both uncertainty and terror as he hears the sound of the wings that signal the approach of the chorus (perhaps envisioning the eagle that is yet to come). And like many mortal heroes in tragedies, Prometheus reveals himself as having acted in full intent but without full awareness of the implications or outcome of his action.

Readers will also note that Prometheus' prediction of the outcome of his struggle with Zeus shifts in the course of the play. In the first half of the play, he anticipates being freed by Zeus in return for a piece of knowledge he holds, and tells the chorus that Zeus "once broken" will be eager to join with him in friendship. The outcome is evidently in Zeus' hands: Prometheus foresees no release except "when it seems good to [Zeus]" and "the mind of Zeus rests from its rage." But he also tells the chorus that Zeus himself is weaker than the fate that finally determines the outcome of things.

Following Prometheus' encounter with Io, we find a shift. He now associates his eventual freedom not with a change of heart on Zeus' part, but with Zeus' fall: "As it is, no limit is set on what I endure / until the day Zeus falls from his tyranny." Prometheus reveals that his secret knowledge concerns a marriage that will result in a son more powerful than his father, and thus in Zeus' overthrow. Zeus will not escape unless Prometheus helps him, after first being released against Zeus' will by one of Io's descendants.

After Io's departure, speaking with the chorus, Prometheus describes Zeus' fall as all but certain: he "will be humbled by the marriage he intends / cast from his tyrant throne, reduced to nothing." There is still the theoretical possibility of Prometheus' helping him ("None of the gods can make it plain to him / how to avoid this anguish: none but me"), but nonetheless, "nothing can prevent / his unbearable failure, his dishonored fall." When the chorus suggest this is merely wishful thinking, Prometheus asserts, "I say what will happen, as well as what I want." And in the final exchange with Hermes, he refuses to disclose his knowledge of the fatal marriage and again asserts Zeus' fall not as a conditional possibility but as a fact.

Prometheus has, then, at different points, offered three visions of the future. (1) Influenced by the knowledge Prometheus has, Zeus will ultimately relent, release Prometheus, and be friends with him again. (2) Prometheus will be released against Zeus' will, and may or may not offer Zeus the knowledge that alone

xvi   *Introduction*

can save him from his fall. (3) Zeus will fall, since no one but
Prometheus can save him, and Prometheus (presumably) will
not do so. Readers may be inclined to agree with Io when she
says, "I can't make sense of this prophecy any more," but the
different versions don't actually contradict each other outright.
Prometheus knows two things: that he will be released by a
descendant of Io's, and that if Zeus makes a certain marriage it
will lead to his overthrow. That fact that the second prophecy
is conditional leaves the nature of its fulfillment uncertain;
Prometheus envisions both the sequence of events and the
outcome differently at different points in the play, depending in
part on his own experience and attitude at that point.

Thus, although the play represents him as a god in a world of
gods, Prometheus is, like the mortal heroes of other tragedies,
not only capable of physical and mental suffering and of loss
but also (in spite of his foresight) subject to the distorting and
obscuring force of emotion, to the ramifying effects of his own
actions, and to the inevitable incompleteness even of prophetic
knowledge.

The Play and the Trilogy

For the reader or audience the last version of Prometheus'
prophecy (which envisions Zeus' fall as unavoidable) presents a
problem of sorts. Greek tragedies may end in ways that are partly
at odds with tradition, but as a rule more radical departures
from familiar myth are only suggested, then corrected by divine
intervention. At the end of Sophocles' *Philoctetes*, for example, it
appears momentarily that the Greeks will fail to capture Troy, but
Heracles arrives to set the story back on course. The prospect of
Zeus' fall, however, is starkly at odds with literary and religious
tradition, which sees Zeus as meeting with various challenges
to his rule but successfully overcoming them. If this play was
written to stand alone, the audience must either suppose a highly
unusual unfolding of events or assume that Prometheus is in part
mistaken in his concluding prophecies.

It is likely, however, that this play did not stand alone, but
was (like all but one of Aeschylus' surviving dramas), part of a

connected trilogy. In fifth-century Athens, writers of tragedies competed at a festival by presenting three tragedies and a satyr play (a short parodic treatment of a mythical subject with a chorus of satyrs). The three tragedies could be on entirely different subjects, as was clearly the norm in the later fifth century, but they could also tell successive parts of the same story, and this is the form that Aeschylus seems to have preferred and may have invented. An ancient commentary on line 524 (513 in the Greek) says that Prometheus was freed "in the next play," and we have good evidence for the existence of a plausible sequel, *Prometheus Unbound*. This drama, to which a number of fragments have been assigned, evidently included a chorus of Titans, now released; it also featured a visit from Heracles, who kills the eagle that is tormenting Prometheus, a prediction about Heracles' future labors, and the release of Prometheus, though the order of these events is unsure. Prometheus' mother, Earth, may also have appeared. It is less clear what the third play was and where it came in the trilogy. Our ancient sources name two other Prometheus plays: *Prometheus the Fire-Kindler* and *Prometheus the Fire-Bearer*. *Prometheus the Fire-Kindler* was almost certainly a satyr play performed with a different group of tragedies. If *Prometheus the Fire-Bearer* is indeed the title of a separate play, and not (as some think) another name for *Prometheus the Fire-Kindler*, it is a play we know almost nothing about; it may well have formed part of a trilogy including *Prometheus Bound* and *Prometheus Unbound*, but scholars are divided about whether it is likelier to have been the first or the last play. If it came last, it may have included the final reconciliation of Prometheus with Zeus, the establishment of a cult, and perhaps the additional civilizing gifts to human beings Plato's dialogue *Protagoras* mentions in its version of the Prometheus story. If it came first (as seems to me more likely) it presumably told the story of Prometheus' theft of fire, never described in detail in our play. *Prometheus Unbound* will in that case have included the concluding events and motifs of reconciliation, gifts, and cult.

The sparseness of our evidence leaves us with unanswered questions about the unfolding of the trilogy, and we may wonder how release and reconciliation could have come about, given the increasing intransigence of Prometheus and the harsh tyranny of

Zeus in our play. Indeed, even if *Prometheus Bound* stood alone and not as part of a trilogy, we would have to envision a similar challenge to the audience's imagination, given the aftermath tradition would lead them to expect. For some critics, the Zeus of this play seems so at odds with the Zeus we find elsewhere in Aeschylus (firmly established and identified with justice and wisdom), and the idea of a changing Zeus so implausible, as to support doubts about Aeschylean authorship of the play (more on this below). But the justice of Zeus is nowhere a simple matter, and what we know of Aeschylus' other trilogies suggests that judgments may alter as circumstances change from one play to the next. Moreover, the very fact that *Prometheus Bound* shows us a divine world still in flux and emphasizes the newness of divine rule should lead us to expect change even in what later may come to seem most stable and invincible.

What makes this particular change hard to envision is the extreme harshness Zeus exhibits in this play. His only supporters are his equally unappealing subordinates (Power, Force, and Hermes), and even they speak only of his power and not of any more engaging or admirable attributes. Prometheus and Io experience his cruelty directly, and Hephaestus, Ocean, and the Oceanids counsel submission primarily for safety's sake. There are, however, indications that should complicate our reading. Prometheus and Zeus are to some extent alike in their inflexibility and bitterness, and if Zeus has acted unjustly, Prometheus too is said to have gone beyond what is right. We have no direct access to Zeus' motives, and we are given at least some prospect of a happy ending for both of his victims.

Some critics argue that this prospect and the ambiguities in the portrayal of Prometheus are among a number of clues that we should from the outset see Zeus as in the right and Prometheus, Io, and the others as mistaken in their reading of his actions.[4] But the fact that the play includes hints of a changed future and of a different understanding of events doesn't mean that we should disregard or trivialize the unhappy present and past it sets before us. The fact that tragedy regularly draws its plots from continuing stories of which we experience only parts in a

4. See, for example, White 2001.

given drama means that the audience may share with characters the experience both of change over time and of belated and retrospective reinterpretation.

Author and Date

Aeschylus is the earliest of three fifth-century Greek playwrights whose tragedies have come down to us from antiquity. He was probably born at Eleusis, near Athens, around 525 BCE. He fought in the Battle of Marathon at the time of the first Persian invasion (490 BCE), and is said to have visited Sicily twice and to have died there on his second visit in 456. His work was first performed in 499; the earliest surviving play, *Persians*, appeared in 472, and the only surviving complete trilogy, the *Oresteia*, in 458. *Prometheus Bound* cannot be securely dated, but is unlikely to have been among his earlier tragedies. Aeschylus may have written as many as ninety plays; we have only seven—or perhaps, only six. I have been speaking of *Prometheus Bound* as an example of Aeschylean tragedy: the play was clearly regarded in antiquity as one of Aeschylus' plays, and survived as part of a selection of seven of his plays. But the authenticity of the play has been questioned since the nineteenth century, and in recent decades close study of stylistic elements has reinforced the view of many scholars that this play (with the rest of its trilogy, if it was in fact part of a Prometheus trilogy) is unlikely to be by Aeschylus.[5] This judgment remains to some extent subjective in spite of the care taken to establish objective criteria; to some (myself included) the tragedy seems like the work of Aeschylus, and to others it doesn't. Those who consider the play non-Aeschylean may be further divided between scholars who think we have an inferior play by a lesser playwright and those who think we have an exceptional play by a (therefore) exceptional but unknown playwright.

---

5. See C. J. Herington 1970; Griffith 1977; M. L. West 1979, 1990; Lloyd-Jones 2003; and the commentaries listed in Further Reading. Some scholars who doubt the Aeschylean authorship of *Prometheus Bound* believe that *Prometheus Unbound*—on this understanding a separate play rather than part of a trilogy—was by Aeschylus.

What features of the play have raised doubts? As I noted above, some find the play's treatment of Zeus inconsistent with that of Aeschylus' other plays. The poetry, although it has a good deal of the grandeur of Aeschylus, is linguistically less complex; the choruses in particular are simpler and less densely metaphorical than in most of his other dramas. Vocabulary, syntax, and meter are in several respects uncharacteristic of what we find in other Aeschylean plays, and various elements in the play seem to point to a later date than is compatible with what we know of the playwright's life and career. The staging seems unusually elaborate and demanding.

It is impossible given our current state of knowledge to be certain about the play's authorship; the fact that we have only a fairly small percentage of Aeschylus' work means that we have to be cautious about generalizations, and the fact that the play was clearly viewed as Aeschylean in antiquity should continue to give us pause. One suggestion that might account both for the play's oddities and for its ancient reputation as Aeschylus' work is that Aeschylus' son Euphorion produced a Prometheus trilogy as the work of his father, perhaps completing an unfinished text. But in the absence of certainty I continue to speak of Aeschylus as the author, not only because this seems to have been unquestioned in antiquity but also because for all the differences scholars have noted, the play seems Aeschylean in its grandeur and scope and in its central thematic preoccupations. Aeschylus' one surviving trilogy, the *Oresteia*, also presents conflicting claims to justice in the context of cosmic evolution; there the protagonists are humans (the Greek general Agamemnon and his family), but the resolution of their intergenerational struggles (through the creation of a law court) is aligned with the final consolidation of Zeus' rule and requires reconciliation among older and younger gods, who take different sides in the human conflict.

Staging

As an explanation for the play's unusual features, some have suggested that *Prometheus Bound* was first performed when Aeschylus was in Sicily.[6] It is more likely, however, that it was (like most fifth-century tragedies) presented at the Theater of Dionysus in Athens, as one of three tragedies followed by a satyr play, on the occasion of the dramatic competition at the City Dionysia, a religious and civic festival in honor of the god Dionysus. The actors, limited to two in our earliest plays and then to three, divided the speaking parts, while the members of the chorus (twelve or fifteen, depending on the play's date), danced, sang, and chanted as a group; the chorus leader also engaged in dialogue with the actors. Chorus and actors were all men, and all wore masks.

The staging of *Prometheus Bound* is particularly controversial. Because Greek tragedies had no stage directions, we have to reconstruct the stage action from what is said in the play and from what we know about performance conditions and practices at the time. But these evolved in the course of the fifth century in ways we can't always date precisely, and in any case we don't know when *Prometheus Bound* was performed. Our uncertainty compounds the problems presented by the play itself. Where was Prometheus? Were the airborne entrances of the chorus and of Ocean and the final cosmic storm simply conveyed to the audience's imaginations by the words of the play, or were they somehow enacted? What exactly happened at the end of the play? I give a brief sketch of the most generally agreed-upon features of the theater as it may have been when this play was produced and of one possible staging among many.[7]

The theater, an outdoor performance space, included an area (the *orchestra*) in which the chorus danced and sang and in which the actors spoke. Behind this area stood the *skene* or stage building, which served as an offstage dressing area for the actors

---

6. For different positions on this issue see C. J. Herington 1967 and Griffith 1978.

7. For further discussion of staging see Taplin 1977, 2003; Griffith 1977, 1983; Conacher 1980; and Davidson 1994.

but might also represent a building or other structure in the play. Actors could enter on either side of the *orchestra* or from a door in the *skene*; they might under some circumstances appear on top of the *skene*. They might also be introduced by means of the *mechane* or crane, used in some plays to represent airborne arrivals or departures, although it isn't certain that this was in use in Aeschylus' lifetime.

From the text of the opening scene we can infer that Prometheus was bound in an upright position; it seems simplest to suppose that he was fastened to something immediately in front of the door of the *skene*, which here stood for the rocky crag. If the chorus' winged arrival was not simply to be imagined by the audience (always a possibility), they could have entered on top of the *skene* in something representing their winged cart or carts. This would make sense both of Prometheus' initial inability to see them and of his eventual request that they come down from the air to continue their conversation with him. Such an entry for the chorus has the further advantage of leaving the *mechane* available for the entrance (and departure) of Ocean, who rides in on a winged creature of some kind.

What then becomes of the chorus and Prometheus at the end of the play? A storm arises, and we have been told that it will conclude with Prometheus' being swallowed up in the earth; the chorus declare their intention of staying with him in spite of Hermes' warnings. In a theater generally devoid of special effects, the vivid language was probably enough to represent the storm; but how did Prometheus and the chorus leave the stage? A staging with Prometheus in front of the *skene* door would allow him to signify his burial by entering the building—either followed by the chorus, if they do stay with him to the end, or by himself if (as some argue) the intensifying storm finally drives them away.

Themes and Images

The Natural World. That this play concludes with a storm is in keeping with the important role in the drama of the natural world. It is often a harsh world: a barren and unprotected landscape of ravines and rocky crags is the site and instrument of Prometheus' punishment; rivers, mountains, lakes, and cataracts, wearisome in their succession and sometimes perilous or difficult to negotiate, mark the stages of Io's wretched wandering; wind, lightning, and thunder presage the final cataclysm. But the natural world can also appear as potentially benign: in his first speech Prometheus responds to his isolation by calling on sky, winds, water, earth, and sun to witness his suffering, and his final words echo this appeal.

Sight. Prometheus' call for witnesses frames the play with another central theme, that of sight. The play suggests several distinctive modes of seeing: to oversee or observe a task in progress, to look on sympathetically, to stare like a mere spectator, to bear witness to suffering, to gaze at an object of desire. Sight, like foresight, is not an unmitigated good. To see is often painful: the chorus, spectators on stage, can at times hardly bear to look at either Prometheus or Io, and Hephaestus similarly finds the imprisoned Prometheus "a sight that's hard for eyes to look at." But the progress of human beings from lives of primitive confusion (with the help of Prometheus) in part entails learning how to use their eyes, a change from the time when although they saw, their sight was somehow useless; vision is indispensable.

Art, Skill, Craft. Prometheus' narrative of human progress (one of several in ancient literature which contrast with the narratives of human decline found in Hesiod's *Works and Days* and elsewhere) emphasizes the acquisition of a series of arts or sciences associated with human civilization: the construction of houses, the domestication of animals, sailing, medicine, arithmetic and writing, the mining of precious metals, and divination. But although these are all seen as benefits, and Prometheus with apparent pride claims responsibility for them, the term for art, skill, or craft (Greek *techne*) is also applied in the play's opening scene to the craft by which Hephaestus imprisons and albeit unwillingly tortures Prometheus: a use that leads him to wish he had not been assigned this role, and even to hate his own skill. Two arts in particular, medicine and the taming of animals, appear both as benign actualities, helpful to humans, and as metaphors for something useless or harmful. The chorus compare Prometheus to a physician unable to heal himself, and Prometheus suggests that it is pointless for Ocean to try to cure Zeus' angry temper or shrink his "swelling wrath"; the medical treatment that is profoundly helpful in the human world thus becomes a metaphor for inadequacy. And the handy domestication of oxen and of horses yields a number of the words (harness, yoke, bridle, bit) that describe the binding of Prometheus and the exile and forced wandering of Io.

Political Power. The despotic rule of Zeus that harnesses Prometheus in place and drives Io from her home is described in the play as a tyranny (*tyrannis* in Greek), and Zeus is a tyrant (*tyrannos*). The term *tyrannos* generally refers to a ruler who has taken power instead of inheriting it (though some tyrants passed power on to their sons) and whose rule is to some degree autocratic. Tyrants and tyrannies varied, and the term could be used in a descriptive rather than a pejorative sense, but Greek literature offers many portraits of tyrants' abuse of power, and in the Athenian democracy of Aeschylus' day popular tradition celebrated (if somewhat inaccurately) the overthrow of an earlier tyranny. In this play, the words are occasionally used in a neutral sense (as, for example, when Power says that Prometheus must "learn to embrace the authority (*tyrannis*) of Zeus" and perhaps when Prometheus himself talks of helping Zeus establish his authority (*tyrannis*). Elsewhere, however, the words *tyrannos* and *tyrannis* regularly evoke the harsh and despotic associations of the English terms.

Speech. Ocean warns Prometheus that because there is a new tyrant among the gods he needs to change his ways, and in particular that he had better watch what he says. Words in this play are sometimes conventionally contrasted with facts or actions, but their power and possible effect are unmistakable. As Prometheus' initial marked silence gives way to a series of long speeches, characters remark that both speech and silence can be painful, that foolish or arrogant words can lead to punishment, and that words can heal. Speech is not entirely in the control of the speaker: both Prometheus and Io feel compelled by their hearers to speak, and as Io leaves the stage in a fit of frenzy she declares that she can't govern her speech. In the concluding scene, however, Hermes warns Prometheus that every word of Zeus will be fulfilled: there is thus in the ruler's case no lack of control and no functional distinction between word and action.[8]

Characters (other than Prometheus)

Power and *Force* are realizations of Zeus' power, bent on enacting Zeus' word; they are divinities with little personality and few attributes separate from the abstractions they personify. The two appear in Hesiod as the offspring of Styx, and Aeschylus' depiction of them as fulfilling Zeus' will without hesitation is very much in accord with Hesiod's description: "These have no house apart from Zeus nor any seat, nor any path except that on which the god leads them."[9] In the *Theogony*, they join their mother in siding with Zeus against the Titans. In accordance with the genders of the two nouns in Greek, Power is male and Force is female; the latter has no speaking part. Hephaestus' comment "Your tongue tells the same story as your looks" suggests that they were frightening to look at.

Hephaestus is the smith of the gods, the god of metalworkers, of craftsmen in general, and of fire. In the *Theogony*, Hera gives birth to him on her own, but here as in Homer he seems to be the son of Zeus. He is represented by both Homer and Hesiod as lame, and may have appeared in this play with a limp. In spite of the fact that it was his own element, fire, that Prometheus stole, he is sympathetic to Prometheus and wretched at having to make use of his skills to maltreat a fellow god. He shared an altar with Prometheus in Athens.

The *daughters of Ocean*, who make up the chorus, are among the many children of Ocean and Tethys; another daughter, Hesione, is named in the play as the wife of Prometheus. In their urgent

---

8. On imagery in *Prometheus Bound* see Fowler 1957 and Mossman 1996.
9. *Theogony* 386–87, translation from Most 2007.

concern for Prometheus the daughters of Ocean have come close to transgressing the usual constraints on young unmarried women: after persuading their father with difficulty to let them go, they rushed from their home without even pausing to put on shoes. They are themselves immortals, but their respect for and fear of more powerful divinities (expressed in their songs) sometimes make them sound very like mortal women. At the end of the play their sympathy for Prometheus and dislike of what Hermes is saying overcomes their timidity and they refuse to abandon the Titan.

Ocean is the river that encircles the earth, and the god who is that river. He is one of the generation of Titans and thus presumably at risk from Zeus, but has not been punished like his brothers, perhaps because of the cautious approach he demonstrates in his conversation with Prometheus. He is eager to help, but somewhat self-important, officious, and prone to judgment. He arrives riding on some kind of four-legged winged creature.

Io is the daughter of Inachus, a river-divinity and child of Ocean and Tethys, which makes the daughters of Ocean Io's aunts. (There are different versions of Io's genealogy but this is the most common.) Aeschylus here omits or downplays certain elements of Io's story. Zeus tries to seduce her; she is turned into a cow, guarded at first by the herdsman Argus, and after his death pursued by a gadfly. After long wanderings she arrives in Egypt, where Zeus restores her original form and she becomes the mother of Epaphos. Io and other characters mention the anger of Hera, but it is never explicitly stated that (as we find in other accounts) her jealousy led to Io's disguise as a cow, that she sent Argus to guard Io, or that Zeus sent Hermes to kill Argus. The geography of Io's wanderings in this play is different from and more complicated than the version we find in Aeschylus' *Suppliants* (which tells the story of Io's descendants, the daughters of Danaus); it is also difficult to be sure of, since some of the landmarks Aeschylus includes appear nowhere else in ancient accounts of geography, and others seem to be located in unexpected places. It has been argued that these oddities point to late and non-Aeschylean authorship; they may, however, simply suggest that the aim here is not geographical accuracy (difficult in any case to attain) but the evocation of a fantastically long and difficult journey.[10]

Hermes is the son of Zeus and the nymph Maia. A trickster figure in his own right in many of the stories about him (notably his theft as an infant of Apollo's cattle), he is here limited to his main role in the Homeric epics, as messenger of the gods. His role in Io's story as the killer of Argus is here suppressed but would probably have been known to the audience. In this play he is essentially Zeus' mouthpiece, impatient with and scornful of Prometheus, and Prometheus makes fun of him as a mere flunky.

Prometheus after Aeschylus

In the *Argonautica* of Apollonius Rhodius, a poet of the third century BCE, the voyage of Jason and the Argonauts (which at times resembles a tour of noteworthy moments and characters in ancient myth) includes a sighting of Prometheus, bound to the rocks by bronze fetters, screaming in anguish as the eagle devours his liver. A survey of post-Aeschylean literature, art, and music offers hundreds of such sightings of the god, as the story is reread and rewritten in different historical and cultural contexts, from antiquity to the present day. A full account of narrations of or allusions to the myth of Prometheus would constitute a kind of history of Western culture, featuring such diverse figures as Aristophanes, Augustine, Voltaire, both Shelleys, Freud, and Marx.[11] The basic elements of the myth (theft of fire, torture by eagle or vulture, creation or acculturation of human beings) tend to recur, but with changes in detail and shifts in emphasis. We also find variations in register, with the tragic Prometheus recast

10. On the geography of Io's route see Finkelberg 1998 and comments and maps in Griffith 1983 and Podlecki 2005.

11. For discussion of the reception of the Prometheus story in art and literature (and for further bibliography on the subject), see Podlecki 2005 and Dougherty 2006.

as a comic figure or a vehicle for satire; only a few decades after *Prometheus Bound*, Aristophanes' *Birds* features a Prometheus who shows up as usual to help human beings, but nervously carries a parasol so the gods won't spot his treachery from above.

Prometheus' association in Aeschylus and beyond with forethought and invention and his solitary resistance and fortitude in suffering have led to his repeated reinvention as allegory, emblem, or archetype; I here offer just a few examples out of many in the literary and philosophical tradition. For the early modern English philosopher and scientist Francis Bacon, drawing on a tradition of similar allegorical readings going back to antiquity, Prometheus signifies Providence at work in human life and thought. For Mary Shelley, author of *Frankenstein: The Modern Prometheus* (1818), he signifies the overreaching scientist, while in Percy Bysshe Shelley's *Prometheus Unbound* (1820), he is "the type of the highest perfection of moral and intellectual nature."[12] The Shelleys' contemporary and friend Lord Byron makes the god an emblem of the human spirit's capacity for endurance and resistance, and the poet Henry Wadsworth Longfellow sees in his gift of fire and his suffering a symbol of the poet as prophet.

For those who focus on the torture Prometheus undergoes, the story's symbolic significance may be personal rather than philosophical or political. In a fragment of poetry by the first-century CE Roman writer Petronius, the vulture is envy and debauchery, at work on the human heart, and Robert Graves, a twentieth-century English writer, makes the tortured god a metaphor for the lover tormented by jealousy. Herman Melville makes a particularly complex use of the Prometheus metaphor in *Moby Dick* (1851): Ahab's obsession with the whale makes him a Prometheus both by virtue of the generative nature of his thought and by virtue of the torment he thus creates for himself.

Perhaps we may see in Franz Kafka's early-twentieth-century sequence of laconic retellings, none more than a few sentences long, an act of resistance to this endless attribution of meaning to the myth. One of Kafka's versions culminates in oblivion (Prometheus' treachery is forgotten by everyone including

---

12. Everest and Matthews 2000, 473.

himself), another in exhaustion (everyone grows weary of the whole meaningless episode). There has, however, been no falling-off in the rewritings of the Prometheus myth or the ascription of meaning to the Titan's struggle, with fresh examples easily found by an Internet search. In 2009 (to take just one example of many), the theatrical company Outside the Wire presented the premiere of its "Prometheus in Prison" project, with readings intended to generate productive discussion among prison employees, at the Missouri Department of Corrections.

About the Translation

This translation, like all translations, constitutes yet another rereading and rewriting of *Prometheus Bound*. My chief aim has been to write a version I would like to teach: one that conveys to readers as much as possible of the poetic and dramatic force of the original and stays close enough to the Greek that the reader's interpretations will be largely founded on Aeschylean thought and expression, though necessarily transformed. I have also tried to produce a translation that can be effectively spoken.

The language of this play is often elaborate, rich in compound adjectives, metaphors, and densely expressive phrasing; it can also be simple and direct. I have tried to convey both modes, but not always by replication of the Greek wording; in aiming for an analogous complexity or simplicity I have sometimes sought Aeschylean effects by other means. And although I have tried to retain the central elements of a given line or passage, I haven't hesitated to transpose these elements where doing so helped me make English poetry out of Greek poetry.

I have tried to avoid the use of obviously old-fashioned or obsolete English. This isn't always easy; to take one example that faces all translators of Greek tragedy, modern English lacks equivalents in the right register for the many exclamations of distress that might once have been translated by "alas" or "woe is me." In rendering these expressions I have either gone with a simple cry of pain or grief ("aah") or have briefly articulated the speaker's response ("what now?" "the pain!"). If, however, I have avoided the archaizing diction that was the norm for translations in the nineteenth and early twentieth centuries, I have followed the example of some other translators (Stanley Lombardo among them) in incorporating into my version phrases from the English poetic tradition, partly in an effort to suggest the presence in the original of traditional poetic diction and of allusion. These quotations are never more than a few words long, and all are at home in modern English, but the reader may catch echoes of Hopkins, Yeats, Milton, Shakespeare, Woody Guthrie, and the King James Bible.

Here as always, the fact that the vocabularies of two languages never map neatly onto each other means that the translator must often choose between giving a word the most appropriate rendering in its context and making accessible to the reader the pattern created by the repetition of that word. The choice is particularly difficult when a word is thematically significant. The Greek word *tyrannis* (tyranny) is sometimes but not always as pejorative as the English word derived from it. The word *techne* can mean craft, art, or skill; the word *sophos* can mean wise, clever, skilled, or ingenious, and can be purely complimentary or slightly derogatory. English and Greek both have a variety of words for seeing, but these variations are not perfectly equivalent. On this issue I have tried for a kind of compromise: I have not aimed at absolute consistency, but where in a particular passage Aeschylus repeats the same word or word family to important effect I have usually translated it by the same English word or a related set of words. Where a word is ambiguous and might be understood in either of two ways, I have in some instances made a choice, but have elsewhere tried to maintain the ambiguity in English or to incorporate both senses in my translation.

Greek meter is based on the alternation of long and short syllables (as English meter is based on the alternation of stressed and unstressed syllables) in different patterns ("feet") and types of line; examples of feet include the iamb (short-long), the anapest (short-short-long), the dactyl (long-short-short), the trochee (long-short), and the spondee (long-long). This play, like other Greek tragedies, includes three different poetic forms: spoken iambic trimeter (three pairs of iambs, with variations) in the dialogue; sung lyric meters (the most diverse of Greek poetic forms) in the choral odes and in some exchanges and solo passages; and chanted anapests at several transitional moments in the play. I have translated the dialogue by a loose iambic pentameter or five-stress line; I have translated the anapests by sequences of shorter lines (including but not limited to English anapests); and I have rendered the lyric portions by a variety of meters, with occasional use of rhyme and near-rhyme, or by free verse. In choral odes, pairs of stanzas (called strophes and antistrophes) correspond metrically; I have attempted to suggest this effect by lines of roughly similar length rather than to replicate it. I have not tried to recreate the sound of Aeschylus' Greek, but in some places where he uses alliterative patterning I have offered such patterning in English; so for example "*horate desmoten me dyspotmon theon*" becomes "you see me fettered, an ill-fortuned god."

I have followed Mark Griffith's text of the play except where indicated in the endnotes. In the few places where the text that has come down to us is obscure or meaningless, I have either followed the emended version that makes the most sense to me or simply offered a comprehensible English reading. The marginal line numbers represent the lines in the English translation; the line numbers at the top of the page refer to the lines in the Greek text.

Acknowledgments

I am indebted to the many scholars who have written on *Prometheus Bound*; Mark Griffith's commentary has been a constant companion, and various editors, commentators, and translators have helped guide my understanding of the play. I have also learned from my students, and in particular from Asher Reisman, whose senior thesis led me to see this tragedy in new ways. Brian Rak has been the most patient of editors; I am grateful to him, to Aryeh Kosman, Sheila Murnaghan, and Seth Schein, and to Hackett's anonymous readers for their many helpful comments, criticisms, and suggestions.

.

Prometheus Bound

Prometheus Bound: Cast of Characters

POWER

FORCE

PROMETHEUS

HEPHAESTUS

CHORUS: DAUGHTERS OF OCEAN

OCEAN

IO

HERMES

SCENE: *A mountainous ravine, with cliffs rising steeply
behind. Enter Power and Force, holding Prometheus
between them, followed by Hephaestus. They place
Prometheus against the rocky wall.*

POWER:

We have come to a distant region of the earth,
the Scythian wilderness where no mortals live.[1]
Hephaestus, you are here to carry out
the commands of father Zeus. Against these rocks,
high cliffs of fall, harness this criminal   5
in chains of adamant, bonds he cannot break.
It was the flower of your own craft he stole,
bright fire, the origin of every art:[2]
stole, and handed to mortals. For this wrong
he must pay the penalty the gods exact,   10
so that he may learn to embrace the authority
of Zeus, and leave his human-loving ways.

HEPHAESTUS:

Power and Force, you've carried out completely
what Zeus decreed; your part in this is done.
But I can't bear to bind a god by force—   15

---

1. The Scythian territory, extending north and east of the Black Sea, would
have suggested to the audience the far north of the known world.
2. Hephaestus is closely identified with fire, and since he is the smith of the
gods, fire is central to his craft.

one of my family—in this wintry chasm.[3]
And all the same I am required to bear it:
it's hard to set aside my father's words.

(He turns to speak to Prometheus.)

Child of Themis who gives sound advice,[4]
20   your thoughts aim high. Against your will and mine,
I'll pin you with bronze chains you can't undo
on this crag far away from humankind,
where you will neither see the forms of mortals,
nor hear their voices. Burnt by sun's bright fire
25   your skin will lose its bloom; you will be glad
when night in spangled clothing hides the daylight,
and again when sun at dawn dispels the frost.
Always the burden of each moment's pain
will wear you down. Your rescuer's not yet born.
30   This is what your human-loving ways have won.
You are a god, and still you did not cower
before the anger of the gods, but granted
mortals honors to which they have no right.
For that, you'll keep watch on this joyless rock,
35   upright, unsleeping, never bending a knee.
You'll cry out often, in sorrow, pain, regret;
it will do no good. Zeus is not to be won over.
He is harsh, as all those new to power are harsh.

POWER:

So—why delay and waste your time on pity?

---

3. Hephaestus and Prometheus are both descended from Uranus (Sky), although they belong to different divine generations.

4. The goddess Themis embodies both what is established and what is right; in this play she is identified with Gaia, the Earth, and is the mother of Prometheus. In Hesiod's *Theogony* (901–6), Themis is the daughter of Earth, a tradition Aeschylus follows in his *Eumenides* (1–3); Hesiod makes her the mother and Zeus the father of the Seasons, Order, Justice, Peace, and the Fates.

Why don't you hate the gods' worst enemy,   *40*
the god who handed mortals your great gift?

HEPHAESTUS:

Family and friendship have a terrible strength.

POWER:

Agreed. But how can you disobey the words
of your father?[5] Don't you fear that even more?

HEPHAESTUS:

You are always unfeeling, always so sure of yourself.   *45*

POWER:

Well, mourning him won't mend things. As for you,
don't make these pointless efforts: they're no help.

HEPHAESTUS:

Oh how I hate this craftsmanship of mine.

POWER:

Why hate it? Here's a simple point: your skill
is not to blame for what he suffers now.   *50*

HEPHAESTUS:

Still, I wish that skill had gone to someone else.

POWER:

Everything's a burden—except to rule the gods;
freedom belongs to nobody but Zeus.

---

5. Zeus, who is Hephaestus' father in Homer though not in Hesiod, and
who is more generally described in both Homer and Hesiod as "father of
gods and humans."

HEPHAESTUS:
I know that now, from this. I have no reply.

POWER:
55   Then why not hurry up and shackle him,
so your father doesn't see you wasting time?

HEPHAESTUS:
The harness is right here, as you can see.

POWER:
Put it around his arms, hammer it in,
use your great power to pin him to the rocks.

HEPHAESTUS:
60   The job is getting done, and no one's stalling.

POWER:
Strike harder, tighten it, leave no slack at all.
He's clever at impossible escapes.

HEPHAESTUS:
This arm is fixed too well for him to loosen.

POWER:
Now secure the other, make him understand
65   that wise as he is, he's dull compared to Zeus.[6]

---

6. The word here translated as "wise" is *sophistes*, originally either a wise person in general or someone who has a particular skill. In the late fifth century BCE, the term was used for professional teachers of rhetoric and other subjects, and began to take on the pejorative connotations of the English word *sophist*.

HEPHAESTUS:

He alone has reason to find fault with me.

POWER:

Now drive the unyielding wedge of adamant
right through his chest, pin him with all your strength.

HEPHAESTUS:

Aah Prometheus, I'm sorry for what you suffer.

POWER:

Holding back again, sorry for those Zeus hates?   70
Watch out: you may soon be pitying yourself.

HEPHAESTUS:

You see a sight that's hard for eyes to look at.

POWER:

I see him getting just what he deserves.
Well, go on, set the bands around his ribs.

HEPHAESTUS:

I'm forced to do this. Don't keep giving orders.   75

POWER:

Oh yes, I'll give you orders, loud and clear.
Go lower, force these shackles round his legs.

HEPHAESTUS:

That job is done. It didn't take me long.

POWER:

80
With all your strength now, pound the fetters in;
the one who oversees this work is strict.

HEPHAESTUS:

Your tongue tells the same story as your looks.

POWER:

Be as soft as you like, but don't go after me
for being rough tempered and inflexible.

HEPHAESTUS:

Let's leave. His body's caught inside this net.

POWER:

(to Prometheus)

85
Here, now, display your arrogance and steal
gods' privileges for creatures of a day.
How can mortals lessen this suffering?
The gods call you Prometheus, Forethinker:
false name. You lack the forethought you require
90
to twist your way out of this work of art.[7]

(Power, Force, and Hephaestus leave. Prometheus,
alone on stage, speaks for the first time.)

PROMETHEUS:[8]

Bright sky and winds as swift as wings in flight,

------

7. These lines pun on Prometheus' name, understood as signifying a person with forethought.

8. In lines 91–220, Prometheus alternates between the meter of spoken dialogue, chanted anapests, and sung lyric meters; the chorus, when they enter, are singing.

flowing streams, and immeasurable laughter
of the sea's tumbling waves; earth, mother of all,
and sun's all seeing eye: I call on you.
See what I, a god, am suffering from the gods.   95

Witness the tortures
that will grind me down
as I wrestle
through countless years of time.
This is what the new leader   100
of the happy gods
has invented for me:
chains and disgrace.
Oh, I grieve at my misery,
now and to come.   105
Where will my suffering end?

But what am I saying? Since I know what will be
in all its particulars, no pain can surprise me.
I must bear my fate as lightly as I can:
the strength of necessity can't be contested.   110
Still I can neither keep silent nor speak out
about what happened. The gift I gave to mortals
has yoked me in these sad necessities:
I hunted down fire's stolen spring and hid it
in a fennel stalk,[9] revealing it to mortals   115
as teacher of all arts, a great resource.
And that's the crime for which I pay the cost,
pinned here in chains beneath the open sky.

Ah no! What now?

What sound, what scent takes flight at me?   120
I can't see: is this a god or a mortal
or a mingled creature? Has it come

---

9. The tradition that Prometheus hid fire in the hollow stalk of the narthex
or giant fennel first appears in Hesiod's *Theogony* (565–67).

to the world's edge here to view my suffering?
Or wanting something else?
125   You see me fettered, an ill-fortuned god:
the enemy of Zeus,
I have earned the hatred
of all gods who enter
the halls of Zeus
130   by my excess of friendship
for mortals. Ah, no!
Again! What do I hear?
A commotion of birds,
as the air rustles
135   with a rush of wings.
Everything that comes near
is a terror to me.

(Enter the chorus, daughters of Ocean,
in winged chariots.)

CHORUS:

[Strophe 1]

Don't be afraid: this is a band of friends,
in winged race to your rocky hill,
140   almost against our father's will:
it was hard, but I won him over in the end.[10]

The quick winds sent me. When the ring
of clashing iron pierced our deep cave,
I didn't care how I behaved,
145   but rushed off, shoeless, on this chariot's wings.

---

10. Although the choruses of Greek tragedy sing and dance as a group, they frequently use the first person singular to refer to themselves.

PROMETHEUS:
Aah. Aah.

Children of Tethys
with her many young,
and of Ocean, who circles
the whole of the earth   150
with unsleeping stream:[11]
look here and see
the fetters that pin me
to this chasm's high crags,
the unenviable watch   155
I will keep.

CHORUS:

[Antistrophe 1]

I look at you, Prometheus, and a mist
of frightened tears comes to my eyes,
to see your body as it lies
here withering against this rocky cliff,   160

misused, in chains you cannot break.
New helmsmen guide Olympus now;
Zeus rules ungoverned, with new law,
and brings to nothing all that once was great.

PROMETHEUS:
If only he had sent me   165
under the earth,

---

11. In Hesiod's *Theogony* (337–70), Tethys and Ocean are among the children of Gaia and Uranus (Earth and Sky) and are themselves the parents of thousands of daughters and sons, including many rivers; the two also appear in Homer's *Iliad*, where Ocean is described as the origin of gods (201).

far below Hades
who harbors the dead,
down to the limitless
170   depths of Tartarus[12]
in cruel chains
that can't be broken,
so no god—or other—
could have gloated at this.
175   As it is, I hang here
swaying in the air,
my pain a delight to my enemies.

CHORUS:

[Strophe 2]

What god is so hard-hearted that he finds
delight in this? Who wouldn't share your sorrow—
180   except for Zeus?
In constant anger and with unbending mind
he subjugates Heaven's children.[13]
He will not stop
until he satiates his heart
185   or someone wins his kingdom (hard to win)
by violence or by art.

PROMETHEUS:

In fact he will need me,
abused though I am

---

12. Hades (properly Hades', that is, the house of Hades) is the underworld realm of Hades, the god of the dead; Tartarus, sometimes identified as a divinity, is a place far below Hades (first mentioned in the *Iliad* at 8.481), and the place where Zeus confined many of the defeated Titans.

13. Progeny of Heaven: the Titans, the older generation of gods, are the children of Uranus (Sky) and Gaia (Earth). The Greek *ouranos* (sky) is here translated as "heaven" to distinguish it from *aither*, which can mean "sky" or "air."

and held in strong fetters.
The lord of the happy   190
will need me still
to reveal the new plan
by which he will be stripped
of scepter and standing.
He will not enchant me   195
with persuasion's sweet charms,
and I will not flinch
at his hard threats
or declare what I know
until he releases me   200
from these cruel bonds
and pays what is due
for this outrage.

CHORUS:

    [Antistrophe 2]

    You are full of confidence, and don't give way
    to bitter agony; you speak too freely.   205
    Side-piercing fear
    provokes my heart to anger and dismay.
    I'm frightened of what may happen:
    when will you see
    the end of trouble, safe in port?   210
    The ways of Cronus' son[14] are out of reach;
    no words can move his heart.

PROMETHEUS:

    I know Zeus is harsh,
    and makes justice his own.
    Still, I think, once broken,   215
    he will prove easygoing,

---

14. Cronus' son: Zeus.

and calm his temper's
rough seas, and come
to join me in friendship,
220   as eager as I am.

CHORUS LEADER:

    Uncover everything and let us know
    the charge on which Zeus seized you. Why does he
    inflict such bitter pain and such disgrace?
    Tell us: unless to tell will somehow harm you.

PROMETHEUS:

225   It hurts me even to speak about these things,
    but it hurts to keep quiet: misfortune on all sides.
    Back when the gods first started to get angry[15]
    and civil war sprang up, one party wanted
    to unseat Cronus and to throw him out—
230   so Zeus could reign, of course—but others urged
    the reverse: that Zeus should never rule the gods.
    I gave the best advice, but failed to persuade
    the Titans, children of Heaven and of Earth.
    They despised my wily schemes, they were so sure
235   it would be no trouble to gain power by force.
    But more than once my mother, Themis, the Earth,
    one being with many names, had given me
    a prophecy of what would come to be:
    that strength and force were worthless, and that those
240   superior in trickery would win.
    But even though I explained this carefully,
    they didn't think it worth consideration.
    Of my alternatives this was the best:

---

15. In Hesiod's *Theogony*, Cronus the Titan first overthrows his father Uranus (Sky) and then tries to prevent his own overthrow by eating the offspring of his wife Rhea. She conceals the last-born, Zeus, who later overthrows his father, though he must still fend off subsequent challenges.

to take my mother with me and join Zeus.
I was a welcome and a willing aide.   245
It's through my plans that Tartarus' dark depths
conceal the ancient Cronus and his allies,
and for my help the tyrant of the gods
has paid me with this wretched recompense.
Tyrants are subject to a kind of sickness: 250
they have no trust in family or friends.
You ask me on what charge Zeus tortures me?
I'll make it clear. As soon as he was seated
on his father's throne, he gave each god a gift,
sharing out power. But the wretched mortals   255
were valueless to him, and so he wanted
to annihilate the entire population
and introduce another in its place.
No one resisted him except for me:
I had the courage, it was I who saved them   260
from being crushed, from going down to Hades.
For that I'm bent by agonies like these,
painful to suffer, pitiful to see.
I pitied mortals, and myself was judged
unworthy of pity. Instead I'm disciplined   265
without mercy, a sight to win Zeus infamy.

CHORUS LEADER:

Only someone made of stone, with an iron heart,
could fail to feel for what you're suffering,
Prometheus. I wish I had not seen it,
and now I have, the pain of it hurts my heart.   270

PROMETHEUS:

Yes, my friends do feel pity when they see me.

CHORUS LEADER:

Did you perhaps go further than you've said?

PROMETHEUS:

I stopped mortals from envisioning their death.[16]

CHORUS LEADER:

What cure did you discover for that sickness?

PROMETHEUS:

275   I brought blind hopes to settle in their hearts.

CHORUS LEADER:

That gift to mortals did them a great service.

PROMETHEUS:

And it was I who gave them fire as well.

CHORUS LEADER:

So creatures of a day have blazing fire?

PROMETHEUS:

Yes, and from fire they'll find out many arts.

CHORUS LEADER:

280   Then it was on these charges Zeus decided—

PROMETHEUS:

to torture me and never let me go.

---

16. A later version of this story appears in Plato's *Gorgias*, where Prometheus is said to have prevented humans from foreseeing the time of their death, not out of pity for their condition, but so that they might be more fairly and accurately judged. There may be an allusion here to the Pandora story as told in Hesiod's *Works and Days*: Pandora, given to mortals by the gods, releases all sorts of evils from the jar she brings with her, leaving in it only hope.

CHORUS LEADER:

Does no end of your struggle lie ahead?

PROMETHEUS:

No end—except when it seems good to him.

CHORUS LEADER:

Seems good to him? What hope is there of that?
Don't you see you went wrong? But saying so   285
gives me no joy and hurts you. Well, let's leave it.
Try to find some escape from this ordeal.

PROMETHEUS:

It's easy, when you've kept clear of disaster,
to give encouragement and sound advice
to those in trouble. But I knew all this.   290
I meant to go wrong. I meant to. I won't deny it.[17]
I helped mortals and found trouble for myself.
Still, I didn't expect a punishment like this:
to waste away against the stony steeps
on this deserted crag with no one near me.   295
But don't lament over my present sorrows;
come down and hear what's going to happen next,
so you can learn it all, to the very end.
Yes: do as I say, and share the suffering
of the latest victim; sorrow's a wanderer,   300
and settles now on this person, now on that.

CHORUS:

We're willing to do
as you urge us, Prometheus,

---

17. The verb here translated as "go wrong" (*hamartano*) has as its most
basic sense "to make a mistake" or "miss the mark." The passage thus
suggests a complicated reading of Prometheus' intentionality.

and now with light foot
305   I leave my swift chariot
and the pure air, the bird's path,
for this stony ground.
I want to hear all
of your troubles.

> *(The chorus leave their carts and prepare to join
> Prometheus on the ground. Enter their father Ocean,
> riding on a winged creature.)*[18]

OCEAN:

310   I have made quite a journey
to come to you here,
Prometheus, guiding
this swift-winged bird
not by bridle and bit
315   but by thought.
And I'd have you know
that I share your pain;
the fact that we're family
obliges me to,[19]
320   I believe, and besides,
I respect no one more.
You may take this as true
since it isn't my way
to flatter. Come now,
325   and indicate, please,
how I should assist you.
You won't ever say

---

18. If the chorus originally entered on the roof of the stage building, at this point they may have descended from it. Since they speak no line in the exchange that follows, and Ocean (their father) never addresses them, it is possible that they came on stage only after his departure.

19. Ocean and Prometheus are both Titans, sons of Gaia (Earth); Ocean is also (as we learn at 563–64) Prometheus' father-in-law.

you've a friend
more steadfast than Ocean.

PROMETHEUS:

What's this? Have you too come as a spectator   *330*
of my suffering? How did you dare to leave
your rock-roofed caverns and your namesake stream,[20]
to travel to this land, the mother of iron?
Have you come here to gaze at my bad luck,
to sympathize and show your indignation?   *335*
Observe this spectacle: the friend of Zeus,
who helped him establish his authority;
see with what agonies he bows me down.

OCEAN:

I see, Prometheus, and I'd like to give you—
subtle though you are—the very best advice.   *340*
Get to know yourself. Change your ways for new ones.
The tyrant of the gods is new as well.
If you toss about such sharp and savage words,
Zeus will soon hear, though he sits far above,
and all this hardship will seem a children's game.   *345*
But, my poor friend, let go your angry mood
and search for a way out of your misery.
What I say here may seem to you old-fashioned,
but still I'll say it: this is the result,
Prometheus, of your too boastful speech.   *350*
You're not yet humble, and you don't give in,
but ask for other troubles on top of these.
So if it's me you take as your instructor,
you won't resist the spur, since you can see
our king's a harsh one, and his rule unchecked.   *355*
And now I'm going, and I'll try and see
if I can release you from this suffering.
Keep yourself quiet and don't talk out of turn;

---

20. Ocean is conceived of as a stream that encircles the world.

or don't you know—since you're so very wise—
360   that a foolish tongue will have to pay a price?

PROMETHEUS:

I envy you because you earn no blame
although you've dared to share all this with me.
Now let it go. Don't bother. In any case
you won't persuade him; he's no easy mark.
365   Make sure your journey doesn't do *you* harm.

OCEAN:

You do much better with advice to others
than to yourself. I judge by facts, not words.
Don't try to pull me back; I'm on my way.
I feel quite sure, I say I feel quite sure
370   Zeus will grant my request and set you free.

PROMETHEUS:

That's good of you; I'll never say otherwise.
You show no lack of thoughtfulness. But still,
don't make the effort. Even if you try,
it will be wasted effort and do no good.
375   So just keep quiet, and stay out of trouble.
If I'm unfortunate, it doesn't mean
that I would want widespread calamity.
Not at all, since I'm already worn with grief
over what has happened to my brother Atlas,
380   who stands in the west and carries on his shoulders
the pillars of heaven and earth, no easy burden.[21]

---

21. In Hesiod's *Theogony*, Atlas is Prometheus' full brother, like him
the son of the Titans Iapetus and Clymene; here he is presumably, like
Prometheus, a child of Uranus (Sky) and Gaia (Earth). In the *Theogony*
(517–18), Atlas holds up the sky; in Homer's *Odyssey* (1.52–54), he holds
the pillars that keep earth and sky apart.

And the earthborn dweller in Cilician caves,[22]
I've seen and pitied him: a dangerous monster,
with a hundred heads, now overcome by force,
furious Typhon.[23] He withstood all the gods,   385
his jaws hissed fear, his eyes flashed dreadful fire,
to raze the tyrant realm of Zeus by force.
Then came the shaft of Zeus that never sleeps,
down from above, the bolt that breathes out flame,
and knocked him from his pinnacle of boasting,   390
struck to his heart, burnt to a strengthless spark.
And now extended long and large he lies
a useless bulk beside the narrow strait,
weighed down beneath Mount Etna's hidden roots.
High on the peaks Hephaestus strikes hot iron,[24]   395
where some day rivers of fire will burst out,
to devour with savage jaws the level fields
of fruitful Sicily. Such is the rage
that Typhon will send boiling forth, hot darts
of fiery spray none can approach, though he   400
was burnt to cinders by the bolt of Zeus.
You've had experience, you don't need me
to teach you. Save yourself as you know how.
I will endure to the end my present fate,
until the mind of Zeus rests from its rage.   405

---

22. Cilicia: in historical times a region on the southern coast of Asia Minor, but in Homer's *Iliad* an area not far from Troy.

23. This Typhon can be identified with the Typhoeus who is represented in Hesiod's *Theogony* as the final threat to Zeus' rule; Earth bears him to Tartarus after the defeat of the other Titans, and his overthrow seals Zeus' victory. Pindar's description (in *Pythian Odes* 1) of his burial beneath Mount Etna in Sicily and the resulting volcanic eruptions is strikingly similar to the account here.

24. Various ancient writers locate Hephaestus' smithy beneath Etna or some other volcano.

OCEAN:

But don't you recognize, Prometheus,
that words can heal a temper sick with anger?

PROMETHEUS:

Yes, if you soften the heart at the right time
and don't use force to shrink its swelling wrath.

OCEAN:

410   Can you see any harm in someone's caring
enough to run the risk? Explain it to me.

PROMETHEUS:

It's useless effort, light-minded silliness.

OCEAN:

Let me suffer this disease, since we gain most
from good sense others think is foolishness.

PROMETHEUS:

415   That failing will appear to be my own.

OCEAN:

Your speech is clearly meant to send me home.

PROMETHEUS:

So your laments for me won't make you hated.

OCEAN:

By the new occupant of the seat of power?

PROMETHEUS:

Watch out for him and for his angry heart.

OCEAN:

Your fate's an education, Prometheus. 420

PROMETHEUS:

Go away, leave, keep to your present purpose!

OCEAN:

You shout at me to leave, but I'm on my way.
My four-legged bird begins to fan the air's
smooth pathway with his wings, and he'll be glad
to bend his knees and settle in his stable. 425

(Exit Ocean, riding his winged creature.)

CHORUS:

[Strophe 1]

I mourn the fate that destroys you, Prometheus.
My cheeks are wet as my soft eyes stream with tears.
Zeus, ruling without restraint, his laws his own,
displays his sharp arrogance to the gods of former years.

[Antistrophe 2]

And now the whole land cries out loud in sorrow. 430
In the westⁱ they mourn the grand ancient honor and glory
you and your brothers shared, and in sacred Asia
mortals share in the anguish of your mournful story:

[Strophe 2]

the girls of Colchis
who are fearless in battle,[25] 435

---

25. The Amazons. Colchis is usually envisioned as east of the Black Sea, but Prometheus later seems to put the Amazons in a different location.

the Scythian masses
around Lake Maeotis,[26]
at earth's far frontier,

[Antistrophe 2]

and the warrior flower
440   of Arabia, whose city
stands high in the Caucasus,[27]
a fierce army, raging
in the clash of sharp spears.

[Strophe 3][ii]

Before now I have seen only one other Titan
445   subdued by the pain of unending imprisonment:
Atlas, the god who carries on his back
the overwhelming strength of the firmament.

[Antistrophe 3]

The waves of the sea cry out as they gather and fall again,
the depths are in mourning, dark Hades groans far within,
450   and the streams of holy rivers mourn your pitiable pain.

PROMETHEUS:

Don't think it's delicacy or stubbornness
that keeps me quiet: my knowledge eats my heart
as I see myself mistreated in this way.
And yet who else but me distributed
455   in full their privileges to these new gods?
No need to speak of that; you know the story.
But listen to the miseries of mortals,
childish until I made them intelligent

---

26. Lake Maeotis: the Sea of Azov.
27. Arabia is here located in the Caucasus, that is, in the general region of the Black Sea.

and capable of thought.[28] I tell you this
not to cast any blame on human beings,   460
but to show the kind intent in what I gave.
At first, they saw but seeing was no use;
they heard but didn't hear. Like shapes in dreams,
they passed long lives in purposeless confusion.
They knew no homes of sun-warmed brick or wood   465
but lived like swarming ants in lightless caves
beneath the ground. They had no way of telling
when winter would arrive, or flowery spring,
or summer with its fruits; in everything
they acted without thought, till I explained   470
the risings and the settings of the stars,
so hard to read. And I did more for them.
I invented number, cleverest of devices,
and writing, hard at work to help recall
all things to memory, the Muses' mother.   475
I was the first to yoke wild animals
as slaves of pack and collar, so they might
take on the weightiest of mortals' burdens;
I harnessed horses to the chariot,
delight of the extravagantly rich.   480
No one else but me invented sailing ships,
that roam the sea with linen wings outspread.
I found all these contrivances for mortals,
but to my sorrow I have no device
by which to escape my present misery.   485

CHORUS LEADER:

Shamed by this treatment, robbed of your good sense,
you've gone astray, and like a bad physician
who has fallen ill, you lose heart, and don't know
how to find out what drugs will cure your sickness.

---

28. Prometheus' narrative includes elements found in other ancient
accounts of human progress toward civilization, such as the one in
Sophocles' *Antigone* (332–72): navigation, animal husbandry, the building
of shelters, and medicine.

PROMETHEUS:

490   Listen to the rest, and you'll be more amazed
       at the arts I invented, the methods I contrived.
       The greatest was this. If anyone fell ill
       there was no defense: no ointment, food, or drink.
       They withered without medicines, until
495   I showed them compounds that would soothe and heal.
       With these they can fend off all sicknesses.
       I set out many systems of divination.[29]
       I was the first to interpret from their dreams
       what would be waking truth; I read for them
500   words hard to decipher, overheard by chance,
       signs met by the road. I carefully distinguished
       the flights of taloned birds: which ones are lucky,
       and which are inauspicious; what they feed on,
       their hatreds, their affections, whom they roost with;
505   the smoothness of the entrails, and the color
       the bile should have if it's to please the gods;
       the mottled surface of the well-formed liver.
       I burnt the thighbone wrapped in fat, I burnt the spine,
       and so led mortals to this unmapped art,
510   clearing the sight for fire's once clouded signs.
       So much for that. As for the benefits
       hidden beneath the earth for human beings,
       bronze, iron, gold and silver, who could claim
       that he discovered them before I did?
515   No one—unless he's fond of pointless chatter.
       One short word sums up all you need to know:
       all human arts derive from Prometheus.[30]

---

29. Ancient methods of divination included the interpretation of a variety
of phenomena: dreams, overheard words or phrases, things encountered
while traveling, the flight and behavior of birds, the entrails of sacrificial
animals, and the way in which sacrifices burnt.

30. Here Prometheus alludes to the significance of his own name (see note
at line 90).

CHORUS LEADER:

Don't offer mortals help out of proportion
and disregard your own unhappiness.
I'm hopeful you will yet escape these chains,   *520*
and once freed, be as powerful as Zeus.

PROMETHEUS:

No: that's not how the fate that brings the end
is destined to complete this.[31] Only when bent
by countless agonies will I escape.
Art is far weaker than necessity.   *525*

CHORUS LEADER:

Who is it, then, that steers necessity?

PROMETHEUS:

The triple Fates and the Furies who remember.[32]

CHORUS LEADER:

So Zeus himself is weak compared to these?

PROMETHEUS:

At least he can't escape from what's in store.

CHORUS LEADER:

What's in store for Zeus, except to rule forever?   *530*

---

31. Fate: here the Greek *Moira*, a word whose basic meaning is "share"
or "portion."

32. Hesiod names three Fates (Clotho, Lachesis, and Atropos), and makes
them the daughters of Zeus and Themis. The Furies, Greek *Erinyes*, appear
sometimes as enforcers of limits or laws, but their chief role (notably in
Aeschylus' *Oresteia*) is to avenge wrongs done by one member of a family
to another.

PROMETHEUS:

You won't find out more: don't keep asking me.

CHORUS LEADER:

It must be some great mystery you're concealing.

PROMETHEUS:

Speak of some other matter. This one's time
has not yet come, but I must keep it hidden
535   as best I can: by guarding it I escape
humiliation, chains, and agony.

CHORUS:

Zeus governs all, and I pray
that his strength will never wrestle against my purpose.
May I never be slow to approach the gods
540   with holy feasts and sacrifices
by my father Ocean's inexhaustible stream.
May I never offend in what I say,
and let this hold good for me, forever unfaded.

Here is something sweet:
545   to draw out a long life in steadfast hope
and feed the heart with gladness.
But I shake with horror to see you,
worn down by sufferings I cannot count.[iii]
No fear of Zeus turns your purpose,[iv]
550   and you revere mortals beyond their due, Prometheus.

Tell me, dear friend, how can their thanks be thanks?
Where is their strength?
What help are those whose life's a passing day?
Did you not see
555   the feeble dreamlike incapacity
that fetters their blind race?
Mortal plans will never evade what Zeus has fashioned.

I learned this as I looked at your ruined fortunes,
Prometheus, and a song
came to me, changed utterly from the wedding song   *560*
we sang by bath and couch
to celebrate your marriage
when you brought home our sister Hesione,
winning her as your wife to share your bed.[33]

*(Enter Io, a young woman transformed into a cow.[34] Her
movements reflect her weariness, her uncertainty, and the
driving presence of the gadfly that pursues her.)*

Io:

What land? What people?   *565*
Who is this I see
in a harness of stone
facing wintry storms?
What was the crime
that called for this death?   *570*
Tell me: where on earth
have I strayed in my grief?

Aah aah the pain the pain.

It stings me again. I am wretched. Aah, the gadfly,
the ghost of earthborn Argus.[35]   *575*
Get him away. Oh no. The terror. I see him,
the herdsman with countless eyes.
He and his shifty look keep pace with me.

---

33. In other sources Prometheus has different wives; here the connection
with Hesione makes him a relative by marriage of the Oceanids, Ocean,
and Io.
34. Io's transformation was presumably indicated by a mask with horns.
35. Argus: the hundred-eyed herdsman sent to watch over Io by Hera
and killed by Hermes at Zeus' command, a story told most fully in Ovid's
Metamorphoses (1.682–715). Io seems to identify the gadfly that now
pursues her with a kind of ghost or image of the dead Argus.

He died but the earth does not cover him;
580   he comes from below to hunt me in my pain,
and drives me starving along the sandy shore.

The pipe of reeds and wax
sings its shrill lullaby.[36]

Ah no, ah no, the pain.
585   I wander far and farther.
Where will my wanderings take me?

What was it, son of Cronus?
What wrong did you find in me
that you yoked me to such pain,

590   aah, aah,

and wear me down,
wretched and frenzied,
in fear of the gadfly's sting?

Burn me with fire
595   or hide me in earth
or give me as food to the beasts of the sea.

Do not refuse my prayers, lord.
I have wandered and wandered again,
worn out by a training too hard.
600   I cannot discover a way to escape this pain.

Do you hear my voice, the voice of the cow-horned girl?

---

36. Here Io may be recalling the panpipes with which Hermes lulled Argus
to sleep so that he could kill him.

PROMETHEUS:

How could I not hear the gadfly-driven daughter
of Inachus, who warms the heart of Zeus
with desire and now is trained by the violence
of Hera's hate to run so long a race?   *605*

IO:

How do you know my father's name?
Tell me, unhappy me, who are you?

Who can it be
whose misery speaks to mine
and tells the truth,   *610*

who names the god-sent sickness
that wastes me, stings me with these wandering barbs?

Aah, Aah,

tormented and starving I rush
in crazy leaps, overcome   *615*
by Hera's vengeful plans.

Of all unlucky beings,
who endures—aah, aah—
what I endure?

Make clear to me   *620*
what suffering lies in wait,
what drug might cure my sickness.
Reveal it, if you know it.

Speak out, explain to me. These are hard travels.

PROMETHEUS:

625   I'll tell you clearly all you want to know,
weaving no riddles, but in simple speech,
open as a person should be with his friends.
You see Prometheus, who gave humans fire.

IO:

You, the common benefactor of all mortals,
630   poor Prometheus, why are you being punished?

PROMETHEUS:

I've just now stopped lamenting my own troubles.

IO:

Then won't you answer as a gift to me?

PROMETHEUS:

Ask what you like; you'll find out everything.

IO:

Tell me who harnessed you in this ravine.

PROMETHEUS:

635   The will of Zeus, but by Hephaestus' hand.

IO:

What are the crimes you're being punished for?

PROMETHEUS:

What I've made clear to you should be enough.

Io:

Tell me also when my wanderings will end:
how long will I endure this misery?

PROMETHEUS:

Not to learn this is better than to learn it.   *640*

Io:

Please don't conceal what I'm about to suffer.

PROMETHEUS:

It's not that I begrudge this gift to you—

Io:

Then why do you hesitate to tell it all?

PROMETHEUS:

From no ill will: I'm afraid I'll break your heart.

Io:

Don't show me more concern than I would like.ᵛ   *645*

PROMETHEUS:

Since your heart's set on it, I'll tell you. Listen.

CHORUS:

Not yet: give me a share of this pleasure too.
Let's ask about her sickness; she can tell us
what chance condemned her to this wandering.
Then she can learn from you what trials remain.   *650*

PROMETHEUS:

Io, it's up to you to do this favor,
especially since they're your father's sisters.[37]
To cry your heart out over what has happened
when you expect to bring your listeners
655   to tears as well is worth the time it takes.

IO:

I don't know how I can refuse you this.
You will learn everything you want to know
in my plain tale; but even to speak of it—
the god-sent storm, what caused the wretched ruin
660   of my appearance—makes me feel ashamed.[vi]
It was nighttime visions, constant visitors
to my bedroom, that kept trying to win me over
with gentle words: "You lucky, lucky girl,
why stay a virgin, when you have the chance
665   to make the greatest marriage? Zeus is inflamed
by the arrow of desire to join with you
in love. Don't reject his bed, child, but go out
to Lerna's deep meadow and your father's herds,[38]
so the eye of Zeus may gain relief from longing."
670   Through all my nights I was wretched in the grip
of dreams like these, till at last I had the courage
to tell my father these night-visiting dreams.
He sent messengers to Delphi and Dodona,[39]
many times, to ask what he might do or say
675   to please the gods. But they returned reporting
answers with shifting words, obscurely spoken,
hard to interpret. At last a clear response
came to Inachus and gave a plain command,
that he should banish me from home and country,

37. Io's father, Inachus, is a river-divinity and thus a son of Ocean.
38. Lerna was a marshy area near Argos.
39. Delphi and Dodona were the two most prominent oracular sites in Greece, the former sacred to Apollo, the latter to Zeus.

set loose to wander at the ends of the earth. 680
And if he should refuse, a fiery bolt
from Zeus would annihilate our family.
Persuaded by Apollo's oracles,
he drove me out and locked the doors to me,
not by his choice or mine: the bit and bridle 685
of Zeus forced him to act the way he did.
My appearance and my mind at once distorted,
a thing with horns, as you see, stung by the gadfly
I ran in maddened leaps toward the sweet stream
of Cerchne[40] and to Lerna's spring. But Argos, 690
the earthborn cowherd with his violent temper
tracked me and kept his many eyes on me.
A sudden and an unexpected fate
deprived him of his life, but I am driven
god-lashed from land to land by the gadfly's sting 695
You've heard what happened. And if you can say
what struggles still remain, then let me know.
Don't—out of pity—comfort me with lies.
A made-up story's a sickness, a disgrace.

CHORUS:

No, no. Keep away. Oh, the pain. 700
I never, never, expected that I would hear
a story so strange
or that things so hard to see and hard to bear—
pain, ruin, fear—
would chill my soul with a double goad.[vii] 705
Fate, Fate, O Fate:
I shudder to see what has become of Io.

PROMETHEUS:

(to the chorus)

Too soon to mourn and to be filled with fear.
Hold out until you learn the rest as well.

---

40. Cerchne: a village near Argos, or the name of a spring.

CHORUS:

710   Tell us everything. The sick are glad to know
in advance exactly what pain lies ahead.

PROMETHEUS:

You easily got what you first asked me for:
to hear her own account of her ordeal.
Now listen to the suffering that remains:
715   what this young girl must still endure from Hera.[41]
You, child of Inachus, take my words to heart,
so you may learn how far your path extends.
First, turning toward the sunrise, make your way
through fields that no one ploughs, until you come
720   to the Scythian nomads, with their homes high up
in woven houses set on wagon wheels.
These archers' bows shoot far, so don't approach them
but pass through, keeping to the sounding shore.
On your left hand the ironworkers live,
725   the Chalybes:[42] you should be on your guard,
since they are wild and don't let strangers near.
You will come to the Violent River,[43] aptly named.
It's hard to cross; don't cross, until you come
to the Caucasus itself, highest of mountains,
730   where the river's strength bursts from the upper slopes.

---

41. In a series of speeches Prometheus now relates both the future and the past wanderings of Io in Europe, Asia Minor, and Africa, and among both human beings and mythical creatures. Some of the landmarks Prometheus mentions appear nowhere else in ancient accounts of geography; others seem to be located in unexpected places. On these oddities, see the Introduction, pp. xxvi–xxvii.

42. The Chalybes were more often described as living on the south shore of the Black Sea; here they appear to be to the northeast, in Scythia.

43. There is no record of a river by this name (Greek *Hybristes*, someone who behaves violently or insolently) and there is no general agreement on which of several known rivers might be meant.

Making your way across star-neighbored peaks,
head southward, where you'll meet the Amazons,
an army that loathes men. Some day they'll settle
by the river Thermodon, in Themiscyra,
near Salmydessus' rugged promontory[44]—   735
unwelcoming to sailors, stepmother of ships.[45]
These women will gladly guide you on your way.
At the narrow gateway of a lake, you'll reach
the Cimmerian Isthmus; leaving it behind,
bravely cross over the Maeotic strait.   740
Mortals will tell forever the grand story
of how you crossed, and call the place Bosporus,
"Cow's Crossing."[46] Here leave Europe, and arrive
on the continent of Asia.

(to the chorus)

                        Don't you think
that in all he does the tyrant of the gods   745
is equally violent? He longed to sleep
with this mortal girl and forced on her these travels.

(to Io)

This was a bitter courtship, girl; the tale
you've just heard isn't even the beginning.

---

44. Aeschylus here reconciles his placement of the Amazons apparently
to the north or northeast of the Black Sea with a tradition that puts them
in the south (at Themiscyra by the Thermodon River) by positing a later
move. But the association of Themiscyra with Salmydessus, traditionally
located in Thrace, remains puzzling.

45. In ancient Greece and Rome, as in the European fairy tale, the stepmother was traditionally cruel.

46. The Cimmerian Isthmus (in modern Crimea) lies between Lake Maeotis
(the Sea of Azov) and the Black Sea; the Maeotic Strait or Cimmerian
Bosporus (understood to mean "Cow's Crossing") connects the two bodies
of water. Elsewhere (for example, in Aeschylus' *Suppliants*), Io is said to
have given her name to the more well-known Bosporus that joins the Black
Sea with the Propontis (Sea of Marmara).

IO:

750   Oh no. Aah. Aah.

PROMETHEUS:

More crying and moaning. I wonder what you'll do
when you learn about the evils that remain?

CHORUS:

Is there any misery left for you to tell her?

PROMETHEUS:

A wintry sea of ruinous agony.

IO:

755   What good is living? Why not throw myself
at once from this hard rock, plunge to the ground,
and escape my struggles? Better to die and be done
than suffer wretchedly through all my days.

PROMETHEUS:

You would find my trials difficult to take,
760   since death's no part of what's in store for me.
That would be a way out of my misery.
As it is, no limit is set on what I endure
until the day Zeus falls from his tyranny.

IO:

And will Zeus really fall from power some day?

PROMETHEUS:

765   You would be glad, I think, to see this happen.

Io:

How could I not be glad, since I'm his victim?

PROMETHEUS:

Go ahead, be happy: what I say is true.

Io:

By whom will he be stripped of the tyrant's scepter?

PROMETHEUS:

By himself and his own empty-headed plans.

Io:

How so? Explain, if there's no harm in it.   770

PROMETHEUS:

He'll make a marriage he later comes to regret.[47]

Io:

With a god or a mortal? Tell, if it can be said.

PROMETHEUS:

Why ask that? It's the part I mustn't speak of.

Io:

It is his wife who makes him lose his throne?

PROMETHEUS:

Yes: she'll bear a child who's greater than his father.   775

---

47. Prometheus is here referring to the story of Zeus' plan to marry Thetis, who later becomes the wife of Peleus and mother of Achilles.

Io:

And there's no way for him to escape this fate?

PROMETHEUS:

None, unless I help him, once I've been released.

Io:

Who will release you against the will of Zeus?

PROMETHEUS:

It's destined to be one of your descendants.

Io:

780   You mean it's *my* child who will set you free?

PROMETHEUS:

Yes: the one born in the thirteenth generation.[48]

Io:

I can't make sense of this prophecy any more.

PROMETHEUS:

Then don't try to learn about your troubles either.

Io:

Don't offer benefits and then withdraw them.

PROMETHEUS:

785   I'll give you one or the other of two stories.

---

48. Heracles.

Io:

Which two? Explain, and then give me the choice.

PROMETHEUS:

I'm giving it. You choose: I can make plain
your remaining struggles or name my rescuer.

CHORUS:

Make her a gift of one, and me of the other.
Don't treat me as unworthy of your story.   *790*
Tell her about her future wanderings,
then tell me what I want: your rescuer.

PROMETHEUS:

Since your heart's set on it, I won't refuse
to tell you everything you want to hear.
First, Io, your far-driven wandering: *795*
write it in the tablets of your memory.
When you cross the stream that bounds the continents,
step toward the fiery rising of the sun,
passing the soundless sea,[49] until you come
to Cisthene,[50] country of the Gorgons; here   *800*
the daughters of Phorcys live, three ancient girls
who look like swans and share one eye, one tooth.[51]

---

49. Soundless sea: this may refer to the Caspian Sea (landlocked and so without the sound of waves), or it may be a riddling expression for the plains Io passes through rather than for any body of water.

50. Cisthene: probably not the city by that name in Pergamum but a region far to the East about which we have no solid evidence; tradition put the Gorgons in a variety of locations.

51. The daughters of Phorcys (a son of the Sea) were known as the Graeae; they shared one tooth and one eye between them. In Hesiod's *Theogony* they are the Gorgons' sisters; they appear in the story of Perseus, who forces them to help him in his quest for the Gorgon Medusa's head. In no other version do they resemble swans, and "who look like swans" here (literally, "swan-shaped") may simply be a reference to their white hair. The Greek word *kore* (here "girl") may be used of unmarried women of any age.

The sun's rays never see them, nor the moon
by night. Their three winged sisters are nearby,
805   the human-hating Gorgons, with snakes for hair.
No mortal who looks at them will breathe again.[52]
I tell you this to put you on your guard.
And here's another hard-to-handle sight:
beware the griffins, the dogs of Zeus that bite
810   but never bark,[53] and the one-eyed mounted troop
of Arimaspians,[54] who live beside
the River of Wealth,[55] whose torrent flows with gold.
Don't go near them. You will reach a far-off land,
a black nation, at the sources of the sun,
815   by the Ethiop River.[56] Follow its banks until
you come to the steep descent where sacred Nile
casts its sweet stream down from the Byblian hills.[57]
Follow this guide to the three-cornered land,
the delta of the Nile, where it is fated
820   you and your children will make a lengthy stay.
If that's at all obscure and hard to grasp,
ask again until you understand precisely.
I have more leisure time than I would like.

CHORUS:

If there's something you've omitted, something left
825   to tell about the wanderings that condemn her,
go on. But if you've said it all, then give us
the gift we asked you for; you must remember.

---

52. There were three Gorgons: Stheno, Euryale, and Medusa. All had the power to turn to stone those who looked at them; Medusa, the only mortal among them, was killed by Perseus.

53. Griffins: creatures like winged lions with an eagle's beak.

54. Arimaspians: a naturally one-eyed people.

55. River of Wealth: this corresponds to no known river.

56. Ethiop river: perhaps the Upper Nile.

57. Byblian hills (or mountains): another unknown landmark. The name seems to refer to the location as a source of papyrus (*byblos* or *biblos*).

PROMETHEUS:

She has heard the whole of her journey, to its end.
But so she knows this was no empty story
I'll say what she went through before she came here,   *830*
giving this evidence to support my words.[58]

(to Io)

I leave out the bulk of the story, and begin
at the very last part of your wanderings.
You had arrived at the Molossian lands
near steep Dodona, the oracle of Zeus   *835*
of Thesprotis, the shrine where oak trees speak
(an unlikely marvel).[59] They addressed you clearly
without riddles, as the glorious wife to be
of Zeus. Does this come back to you with pleasure?
Then in a frenzy by the seaside path   *840*
you rushed along toward the great gulf of Rhea,[60]
storm-driven back along your course again.
You can be sure that a recess of the sea
will in times to come be called Ionian,
a reminder to all mortals of your crossing.   *845*
This is your proof that my intelligence
perceives more than is openly revealed.

(to the chorus)

The rest I'll tell to you and her together,
returning to the track of my earlier story.

---

58. Greek seers typically knew the past as well as the present and future, and might use their knowledge of the past to confirm their mantic powers; see Cassandra's words in Aeschylus' *Agamemnon* (1194–97).

59. The Molossian plain is in northwestern Greece. Dodona was the most important oracle on mainland Greece after Delphi, sacred to Zeus as Delphi was to Apollo; Zeus' will and his predictions were made known through the rustling of oak trees. Thesprotis is a region in northwestern Greece.

60. Gulf of Rhea: the Adriatic Sea.

850   There's a city, Canopus,[61] at the edge of the land,
       by the Nile's mouth, where the river drops its silt.
       There Zeus will bring you to your senses, with
       a gentle touch, a hand you need not fear.
       Your son, dark Epaphus, born from that touch
855   and named for it, will harvest all the land
       irrigated by the broadly flowing Nile.[62]
       Five generations later his descendants,
       fifty daughters, will return unwillingly
       to Argos, fleeing a marriage to their cousins,[63]
860   who follow, hearts roused, like hawks after doves,
       hunting forbidden marriage; a god will deny them
       the bodies they desire. Pelasgus' country
       will be steeped in war where women are the killers,
       boldly watching at night to subdue their men.
865   A wife will rob each husband of his life,
       dipping her two-edged sword in streams of blood.
       I hope love comes to my enemies in this way.
       But desire will work its charm on one of the girls:
       she will not kill her husband, but will blunt
870   her purpose, of two courses choosing one:
       to be called cowardly rather than murderous.
       She will give birth to the Argive royal family.
       It would take too long to set it out in detail,
       but from this seed a brave man will be born,
875   famed for his bow, and he will rescue me.[64]
       This is the prophecy my ancient mother,

---

61. Canopus: a city in the Nile delta, near the later site of Alexandria.

62. The name Epaphus is treated as a pun on the verb *epaphao*, meaning "to touch lightly." Io's son is sometimes identified with the Egyptian god Apis, who took the form of a bull.

63. This passage refers to the story of the Danaids (daughters of Danaus); Aeschylus' *Suppliants* tells about their flight from their cousins and would-be husbands and their appeal to Pelasgus, king of Argus, for refuge. The lost plays of the trilogy continued the story and seem to have included the murder of all of the sons of Egyptus but one and the trial of the one sister, Hypermestra, who spared her husband.

64. The man famed for his bow is Heracles.

Themis, mother of Titans, recounted to me,
but how it will happen would take too long to tell
and you would gain nothing from the information.

Io:

On, on, on, on!   *880*
Again wrung by pain,
on fire with the madness
that beats on my mind,
stung by the gadfly,
a barb no man forged.   *885*
My heart kicks my chest
in fear, my eyes roll.
The fierce breath of frenzy
drives me off course.
I can't govern my tongue.   *890*
Troubled words strike at random
on the waves
of hateful disaster.

(Her pain once again driving her, Io rushes from the stage.)

Chorus:

[Strophe 1]

He was wise, he was wise,
who first gave thought to this and spoke it out: *895*
to marry where you belong is best by far.
If you are poor don't set your heart on marriage
with those who luxuriate in wealth
or pride themselves on family.

[Antistrophe 1]

Never, never, long-lived Fates,[viii]   *900*
may you see me sharing the bed of Zeus.

No marriage with one of the heavenly sort for me.
I'm frightened when I see Io,
a virgin who shunned a husband,
905   destroyed by Hera's hard traveling.

[Epode]

When marriage is like to like,
I'm not afraid. But I fear this: that the desire[ix]
of stronger gods should ever direct
an inescapable gaze at me,
910   a fight that can't be fought, a way with no way out.
I don't know what would become of me.
I don't see how I could escape the cunning of Zeus.

PROMETHEUS:
Still: stubborn as he is, I say that Zeus
will be humbled by the marriage he intends,
915   cast from his tyrant throne, reduced to nothing.
The curse his father Cronus spoke as he fell
from his long-held throne will be realized in full.[65]
None of the gods can make it plain to him
how to avoid this anguish: none but me.
920   I know the what and the how. In face of this
let him sit boldly, trusting in the thunder
on high as he brandishes his fire-breathing bolt.
Nothing will help him, nothing can prevent
his unbearable failure, his dishonored fall.
925   Such is the challenger he's making ready
for himself, a marvel difficult to fight,
who will find a flame more powerful than lightning,
with a noise that overwhelms the thunderclap,
and will break to bits the trident of Poseidon,

---

65. Cronus' curse is mentioned nowhere else.

earth-shaking sea spear.[66] Dashed against this evil,   930
Zeus will learn how far rule is from slavery.[x]

CHORUS:

You threaten Zeus with what you're longing for.

PROMETHEUS:

I say what will happen, as well as what I want.

CHORUS:

Should we expect that Zeus will find a master?

PROMETHEUS:

Yes: he'll have troubles worse to bear than mine.   935

CHORUS:

Why aren't you afraid to say such words out loud?

PROMETHEUS:

What should I fear? It's not my fate to die.

CHORUS:

He might send some still more painful trial than this.

PROMETHEUS:

Let him do it, then. I'm prepared for everything.

---

66. Prometheus envisions the son who will result from Zeus' ill-advised marriage to the unnamed Thetis. The mention of the trident, emblem of Poseidon, recalls the version of the story (told by Pindar) in which Zeus and Poseidon compete for Thetis and are both warned off.

CHORUS:

940   Those who bow down to Necessity are wise.[67]

PROMETHEUS:

Worship, pray, fawn on whoever is in power;
to me Zeus matters less than nothing at all.
Let him act, let him hold power for this short time
as he likes. He will not rule the gods for long.

945   But I see the errand boy of Zeus is here—
the menial who waits on our new tyrant.
He must have come to bring some fresh report.

(Enter Hermes, the messenger of Zeus.)

HERMES:

You, the wise one, bitter and more than bitter,
the one who wronged the gods in furnishing
950   honors to mortals, I mean the thief of fire:
my father orders you to name this marriage,
the one you boast will make him fall from power.
What's more, he tells you not to speak in riddles,
but say things as they are. Don't burden me
955   with a second trip, Prometheus. You see,
Zeus isn't softened by such ways as yours.

PROMETHEUS:

A solemn speech, and full of arrogance,
suitable for a servant of the gods!
You are young, and young in power, and so you think
960   you live in citadels beyond all sorrow.
Wasn't it from these citadels I saw

---

67. Necessity: Greek *Adrasteia*, literally "the Inescapable," one of the names of Nemesis, the personification of divine retribution.

two tyrants fall?[68] And I will see a third,
our present ruler, fall most disgracefully
and very soon. Do I really seem to you
to dread these new gods and to cower before them?   *965*
I am as far from that as I can be.
So hurry back again the way you came;
you will get none of what you ask me for.

HERMES:

    It was by just such acts of stubbornness
    you brought yourself to anchor in this pain.   *970*

PROMETHEUS:

    You can be sure of this: I wouldn't exchange
    my own misfortune for your servitude.

HERMES:

    I suppose it's better to be a slave to this rock,
    than Zeus my father's trusted messenger.

PROMETHEUS:

    This is the way to insult the insolent.[xi]   *975*

HERMES:

    You seem to luxuriate in your present state.

PROMETHEUS:

    Luxuriate? I'd like to see my enemies
    luxuriate like this, and you among them.

HERMES:

    Do you somehow blame me too for your misfortunes?

---

68. Two tyrants: Uranus and his son Cronus.

PROMETHEUS:

980   To put it simply: I hate all the gods,
who do me wrong although I did them good.

HERMES:

To me you sound more than a little sick.

PROMETHEUS:

Perhaps, if it's sick to hate one's enemies.

HERMES:

Who could put up with you if you were happy?

PROMETHEUS:

985   Aah.

HERMES:

There's an expression Zeus doesn't understand.

PROMETHEUS:

But time as it grows old teaches everything.

HERMES:

And still you haven't yet learned self-control.

PROMETHEUS:

True, or I wouldn't be talking with a servant.

HERMES:

So you'll tell my father none of what he wants.

PROMETHEUS:

Of course, I should pay him back: I'm in his debt! 990

HERMES:

You're mocking me as if I were a child.

PROMETHEUS:

Aren't you a child, and more mindless than a child,
if you expect to learn anything from me?
There is no torment, no device by which
Zeus will persuade me to say a word of this 995
till he undoes these fetters that defile me.
In face of my defiance let him throw
his blazing fire, and disrupt all the world
with thundering earthquakes and white-feathered snow.
None of this can bend my will and make me say 1000
at whose hands he must fall from his tyranny.

HERMES:

Well, see if this seems to do you any good.

PROMETHEUS:

It has long ago been seen to and decided.

HERMES:

Your behavior's pointless. Bring yourself at last
to think straight, faced with your present misery. 1005

PROMETHEUS:

This is pointless harassment: as well advise the sea.
Don't suppose that in my fear of what Zeus plans
I will come to think as females do, and beg
the one I hate so much, my hands held out
like a suppliant woman's, to set me free: far from it! 1010

HERMES:

It seems that more talk will be pointless talk.
You are not softened by my pleas at all,
and like a newly harnessed colt you take
the bit in your teeth to fight against the reins.

1015   But your vehemence rests on an unsound theory,
since stubbornness in someone who's unable
to reason well is utterly powerless.
But if you're not persuaded by my words,
think what a storm is coming: wave on wave

1020   of inescapable evils. First, my father
will crack this rugged chasm apart with thunder
and lightning flame and hide away your body,
gripped in a stone embrace. Then, at the end
of a long, long time, you'll come back to the light,

1025   and the winged hound of Zeus, the blood-red eagle,
will fiercely carve your body into shreds,
coming uninvited, a daylong dinner guest,
and feast on your liver, bitten dark with blood.
Expect no limit to such suffering

1030   until some god proves willing to take on
your struggles and descend to sunless Hades
and the murky depths of Tartarus.[69] Plan on this:
it's no fictitious threat but all too true.
The mouth of Zeus does not know how to lie

1035   but accomplishes each word. So look around,
and give it careful thought, and don't suppose
that stubbornness is better than sound advice.

CHORUS:

To us what Hermes says seems to the point.
He's telling you to let go your stubbornness

---

69. The god who takes Prometheus' place might be either the centaur
Chiron, who gives up his immortality to end his suffering from a wound,
or Heracles, who travels to the underworld.

and search for wise advice instead. Give in!   *1040*
When someone wise goes wrong, it's a disgrace.

PROMETHEUS:

It's well known to me,
this news he proclaims.
But from those you hate
hurt has no shame.   *1045*
So be thrown at me,
forked coil of fire.
Thunder rouse sky
in the throes of wild winds.
Wind shake the earth,   *1050*
roots and all, to its base.
Let surging sea's
savage breakers confound
the stars in their courses,
lift me and throw me   *1055*
down to Tartarus, trapped
in necessity's whirl.
Even so:
he won't put *me* to death.

HERMES:

Such resolve, such talk,   *1060*
you can hear from the crazed.
How does this boasting
differ from lunacy?
Is it any less mad?

(to the chorus)

And you, who share in   *1065*
his misery: quick,
get away from this place,
before thunder's roar
shocks you senseless.

CHORUS:

1070   Say something else;
urge a course that persuades me,
since I can't endure
this unasked-for advice.
How can you order me
1075   to act like a coward?
I am willing to suffer
with him as I must.
I have learned this lesson:
to hate all traitors.
1080   I despise no disease
more than this.

HERMES:

Well, do bear in mind
my warning to you:
don't blame your luck
1085   when disaster comes hunting,
and don't say Zeus cast you
into unforeseen misery.
No: you yourselves did it
to yourselves. With full knowledge,
1090   not in secret, not suddenly,
your folly will snare you
in disaster's inescapable net.

(Exit Hermes; the chorus remain, at Prometheus' feet,
as the storm begins and intensifies.)

PROMETHEUS:

And now in fact
no longer in word
1095   the earth is shaken.
The roar of thunder
replies from the depths.

Fiery coils
of lightning flash forth,
dust eddies and wheels,   *1100*
every gust of wind leaps
to contend with another
in angry display.
Sea is stirred up
and mingled with sky.   *1105*
This onslaught from Zeus
comes at me openly
to fill me with fear.
O my revered mother,[70]
O sky, whose encircling   *1110*
light we all share,
you see:
how unjustly I suffer!

---

70. In addressing his mother, Prometheus also addresses the earth, as he did
in his opening words.

Endnotes

Here I note departures from the text of Griffith's edition (Griffith 1983) and a few other textual issues.

i. 431 (409 in the Greek): "in the west." Here I have accepted Wecklein's suggested supplement (noted by Griffith) for an evident lacuna (a gap in the received text).

ii. 444–47 (425–30 in the Greek): these lines have a number of difficulties in meter, style, and meaning; see Griffith.

iii. 548 (541 in the Greek): there is a lacuna at the end of this line; in this case I haven't included any of the supplements scholars have proposed.

iv. 549 (543 in the Greek): part of this line is metrically problematic (see Griffith) but I have translated the Greek (loosely) as it stands.

v. 645 (629 in the Greek): the idiom here is a debated one; my translation follows a different punctuation (and a different understanding of the line) from that in Griffith.

vi. 660 (642 in the Greek): here I follow editions that adopt the reading *aischunomai* (I am ashamed), found in some manuscripts, rather than *oduromai* (I weep), found in others and preferred by Griffith.

vii. 704–5 (691–92 in the Greek): meter and syntax are problematic; I follow Griffith's understanding of the general sense rather than accepting any particular emendation.

viii. 900 (895 in the Greek): here I accept Hermann's supplement (noted by Griffith) for the lacuna.

ix. 905, 907 (900, 901–2 in the Greek): there are textual problems in these lines; I have gone with what seems a plausible understanding of the general sense.

x. 930–31 (924 in the Greek): I have omitted the word *nosos* (sickness), identified by Griffith as suspect, but have not supplied an alternative.

xi. 975 (970 in the Greek): Griffith, with other editors, assumes a lacuna of at least one line before this line, chiefly because it doesn't seem to make sense as a response to what Hermes has just said.

Further Reading

This list of suggested readings is limited to a small selection of fairly recent scholarship written in or available in English. For additional bibliography, see Conacher, Griffith, Podlecki, and Sommerstein.

Texts, Commentaries, and Translations

Collard, Christopher, trans. and comm. 2008. *Aeschylus: Persians and Other Plays.* Oxford: Oxford University Press.

Conacher, D. J. 1980. *Aeschylus' Prometheus Bound: A Literary Commentary.* Toronto: University of Toronto Press.

Grene, David, trans. 2012. *Aeschylus: Prometheus.* In *The Complete Greek Tragedies*, vol. 1, *Aeschylus*, edited by D. Grene and R. Lattimore; rev. 3rd ed. by M. Griffith and G. W. Most. Chicago: University of Chicago Press. Original version published 1956.

Everest, Kelvin, and Geoffrey Matthews, eds. 2000. *The Poems of Shelley*, vol. 2. Harlow: Longmans.

Griffith, Mark, ed. and comm. 1983. *Aeschylus: Prometheus Bound.* Cambridge: Cambridge University Press.

Herington, C. John, and James Scully, trans. and comm. 1975. *Aeschylus: Prometheus Bound.* Oxford: Oxford University Press.

Matthews, William, trans. 1999. *Prometheus Bound.* In *Aeschylus*, 2, edited by D. R. Slavitt and P. Bovie. Philadelphia: University of Pennsylvania Press.

Most, Glenn W., ed. and trans. 2007. *Hesiod: Theogony, Works and Days, Testimonia.* Cambridge, MA: Harvard University Press.

Podlecki, A. J., ed., trans., and comm. 2005. *Aeschylus: Prometheus Bound*. Oxford: Aris & Phillips.

Raphael, Frederic, and McLeish, Kenneth, trans. 1991. *Prometheus Bound*. In *Aeschylus, Plays: One*, translated by F. Raphael and K. McLeish, edited by J. M. Walton. London: Methuen.

Sommerstein, Alan H., ed. and trans. 2008. *Aeschylus: Persians, Seven against Thebes, Suppliants, Prometheus Bound*. Cambridge, MA: Harvard University Press.

Books and Articles

Davidson, John. 1994. "'Prometheus Vinctus' on the Athenian Stage." *Greece & Rome* 41: 33–40.

Dodds, E. R. 1973. "The *Prometheus Vinctus* and the Progress of Scholarship." In E. R. Dodds, *The Ancient Concept of Progress and other Essays on Greek Literature and Belief*, 26–44. Oxford: Clarendon.

Dougherty, Carol. 2006. *Prometheus*. London: Routledge.

Finkelberg, Margalit. 1998. "The Geography of the *Prometheus Vinctus*." *Rheinisches Museum für Philologie* 141: 119–41.

Fowler, B. H. 1957. "The Imagery of the *Prometheus*." *American Journal of Philology* 78: 173–84.

Gagarin, Michael. 1976. *Aeschylean Drama*. Berkeley: University of California Press.

Griffith, Mark. 1977. *The Authenticity of Prometheus Bound*. Cambridge: Cambridge University Press.

Griffith, Mark. 1978. "Aeschylus, Sicily, and Prometheus." In *Dionysiaca: Nine Studies in Greek Poetry, Presented to Sir Denys Page on His Seventieth Birthday*, edited by R. D. Dawe, J. Diggle, and P. E. Easterling, 105–39. Cambridge: Cambridge University Library.

Herington, C. J. 1967. "Aeschylus in Sicily." *The Journal of Hellenic Studies* 87: 74–85.

Herington, C. J. 1970. *The Author of the Prometheus Bound*. Austin: University of Texas Press.

Herington, John. 1986. *Aeschylus*. New Haven: Yale University Press.

Lloyd-Jones, Hugh. 2003. "Zeus, Prometheus, and Greek Ethics." *Harvard Studies in Classical Philology* 101: 49–72.

Mossman, J. M. 1996. "Chains of Imagery in *Prometheus Bound*." *Classical Quarterly* n.s. 46: 58–67.

Rosenmeyer, Thomas G. 1982. *The Art of Aeschylus*. Berkeley: University of California Press.

Scott, William C. 1987. "The Development of the Chorus in *Prometheus Bound*." *Transactions of the American Philological Association* 117: 85–96.

Sommerstein, Alan H. 2010. *Aeschylean Tragedy*, 2nd ed. London: Duckworth.

Taplin, Oliver. 1977. *The Stagecraft of Aeschylus: The Dramatic Use of Exits and Entrances in Greek Tragedy*. Oxford: Clarendon.

Taplin, Oliver. 2003. *Greek Tragedy in Action*, 2nd ed. London: Routledge.

Vernant, Jean-Pierre. 1980. "The Myth of Prometheus in Hesiod." In *Myth and Society in Ancient Greece*, edited by J.-P. Vernant, translated by J. Lloyd. Brighton: Harvester Press. Originally published in 1974 as *Mythe et Société en Grèce Ancienne* (Paris: Maspero).

West, M. L. 1979. "The Prometheus Trilogy." *Journal of Hellenic Studies* 99: 130–48. Reprinted with a postscript in M. Lloyd, ed. 2007. *Aeschylus*. Oxford: Oxford University Press.

West, M. L. 1990. "The Authorship of the Prometheus Triology." In *Studies in Aeschylus*, edited by M. L. West, 51–72. Stuttgart: Teubner.

West, Stephanie. 1994. "Prometheus Orientalized." *Museum Helveticum* 51: 129–49.

White, Stephen H. 2001. "Io's World: Intimations of Theodicy in *Prometheus Bound*." *Journal of Hellenic Studies* 121: 107–40.

Winnington-Ingram, R. P. 1983. *Studies in Aeschylus*. Cambridge: Cambridge University Press.